NVA STUDIOS

100 Iconic Buildings with Unique Design and Architecture

Copyright © 2023 by NVA STUDIOS

All rights reserved. No part of this publication may be reproduced, stored or transmitted in any form or by any means, electronic, mechanical, photocopying, recording, scanning, or otherwise without written permission from the publisher. It is illegal to copy this book, post it to a website, or distribute it by any other means without permission.

First edition

This book was professionally typeset on Reedsy. Find out more at reedsy.com

Contents

1	Great Pyramid of Giza, Egypt	1
2	Taj Mahal, India	3
3	Eiffel Tower, France	5
4	Colosseum, Italy	7
5	Sydney Opera House, Australia	10
6	Statue of Liberty, USA	13
7	Burj Khalifa, UAE	15
8	Parthenon, Greece	18
9	Machu Picchu, Peru	21
10	Saint Basil's Cathedral, Russia	24
11	Sagrada Família, Spain	27
12	Forbidden City, China	30
13	Angkor Wat, Cambodia	33
14	Westminster Abbey, UK	36
15	Petra, Jordan	39
16	Christ the Redeemer, Brazil	42
17	Leaning Tower of Pisa, Italy	45
18	Neuschwanstein Castle, Germany	48
19	Alhambra, Spain	51
20	Hagia Sophia, Turkey	54
21	Louvre Museum, France	57
22	Potala Palace, Tibet	60
23	Chichen Itza, Mexico	63
24	Brandenburg Gate, Germany	66
25	Tower Bridge, UK	69
26	Golden Gate Bridge, USA	72

27	Shard, UK	75
28	CN Tower, Canada	78
29	Pyramids of Teotihuacan, Mexico	81
30	Kremlin, Russia	84
31	Sydney Harbour Bridge, Australia	87
32	Mont Saint-Michel, France	90
33	Great Wall of China, China	93
34	Grand Central Terminal, USA	96
35	Petronas Towers, Malaysia	99
36	The White House, USA	102
37	Big Ben, UK	105
38	St. Peter's Basilica, Vatican City	108
39	The Guggenheim Museum Bilbao, Spain	111
40	Taipei 101, Taiwan	114
41	The Parthenon, USA	118
42	Marina Bay Sands, Singapore	121
43	Guggenheim Museum, USA (New York)	124
44	The Atomium, Belgium	127
45	Lotus Temple, India	130
46	Casa Milà, Spain	133
47	Empire State Building, USA	136
48	Willis Tower (formerly Sears Tower), USA	139
49	Buckingham Palace, UK	143
50	Milan Cathedral, Italy	146
51	Palace of Westminster, UK	150
52	Versailles Palace, France	153
53	Rila Monastery, Bulgaria	156
54	Burj al-Arab, UAE	159
55	Metropol Parasol, Spain	162
56	Gateway Arch, USA	165
57	World Trade Center, USA	168
58	Tower of David, Israel	171
59	Alcatraz Island, USA	174

60	Blue Mosque, Turkey	177
61	Sydney Tower Eye, Australia	180
62	Paul's Cathedral, UK	183
63	Palace of Culture and Science, Poland	186
64	Lotte World Tower, South Korea	189
65	Montparnasse Tower, France	192
66	International Commerce Centre, Hong Kong	195
67	Tokyo Skytree, Japan	198
68	The Great Sphinx of Giza, Egypt	201
69	Moai Statues, Easter Island	204
70	Cappadocia Cave Churches, Turkey	207
71	Trevi Fountain, Italy	210
72	Victoria Falls Bridge, Zambia/Zimbabwe	213
73	Stonehenge, UK	216
74	Wat Rong Khun (White Temple), Thailand	219
75	Rialto Bridge, Italy	222
76	Edinburgh Castle, UK	225
77	Space Needle, USA	228
78	Museum of the Future, UAE	231
79	Borobudur, Indonesia	234
80	Gardens by the Bay, Singapore	237
81	The Milan Cathedral (Duomo di Milano), Italy	240
82	The Chrysler Building, USA	243
83	National Monument, Indonesia	246
84	Kota Tua, Indonesia	249
85	Bellagio Hotel & Casino, USA	251
86	Hudson Yards, USA	253
87	Rockefeller Center, USA	255
88	9/11 Memorial & Museum, USA	259
89	One Vanderbilt, USA	261
90	TCL Chinese Theatre, USA	264
91	Griffith Observatory, USA	266
92	Tokyo Tower, Japan	268

93	Macau Tower Convention and Entertainment Center, China	270
94	Dubai Frame, UAE	272
95	Transamerica Pyramid, USA	275
96	Coit Tower, USA	278
97	The Gherkin, UK	280
98	The Cathedral of Brasília	282
99	Shanghai World Financial Center, China	284
100	Fairmont Le Château Frontenac, Canada	287

1

Great Pyramid of Giza, Egypt

Standing proudly in the heart of Egypt's vast desert landscape is a timeless masterpiece that echoes the whispers of ancient civilizations – the Great Pyramid of Giza. As the oldest and grandest of the Seven Wonders of the Ancient World, this colossal structure is a testament to the ingenuity and ambition of the human spirit.

Imagine the world as it was thousands of years ago – a time when engineering marvels were forged not with computers but with grit, sweat, and an unquenchable thirst for understanding the universe. The Great Pyramid was constructed over 4,500 years ago during the reign of Pharaoh Khufu, a towering monument that reaches for the heavens, each of its mammoth limestone blocks placed with precision that modern architects still marvel at.

But beyond its monumental size lies a design shrouded in mystique and ancient wisdom. The pyramid's sides align with the cardinal points of the compass, a connection to the cosmos that evokes a sense of human yearning to bridge the earthly and the celestial. The mathematical precision and astronomical alignment of the pyramid reveal the ancient Egyptians' deep-rooted knowledge of the cosmos, as if they were striving to touch the realm of the gods themselves.

Picture the labor of thousands, the dedication of generations, all to create a monument that was more than just a tomb. It stood as a symbol of a civilization's power, an expression of belief in the afterlife, and a beacon of architectural innovation that still astounds today. The Great Pyramid was an audacious feat, a challenge flung at the face of nature itself – a declaration that humanity's curiosity knows no bounds.

And as history winds its way through millennia, the Great Pyramid of Giza continues to captivate. Its sheer presence humbles those who stand before it, inviting contemplation about the mysteries of time, creation, and the endurance of human creativity. This towering sentinel is more than a monument; it's a bridge that connects us to the very essence of our past, a reminder that the human spirit can forge marvels that defy the ages and that inspiration can rise from the sands of time.

2

Taj Mahal, India

Amidst the enchanting landscapes of India, there exists a symphony in marble, a testament to eternal love – the Taj Mahal. This ethereal masterpiece stands not only as an architectural marvel but as a poignant reminder that human creativity can transcend time, cultural boundaries, and even mortality itself.

Picture yourself transported to the 17th century, a time when empires rose and fell like tides, and hearts danced to the rhythms of romance. The Taj Mahal was born from the heartache of Emperor Shah Jahan, who, in the wake of his wife Mumtaz Mahal's passing, sought to immortalize their love in the most exquisite way possible. It was not merely a mausoleum; it was a fervent promise etched in marble, a declaration of devotion that transcends the ages.

The Taj's architectural poetry unfolds like a tale spun by the winds of history. Its design is a harmonious fusion of Persian, Islamic, and Indian influences, a symphony of artistic languages that mirrors the tapestry of India's rich heritage. The minarets that frame its luminous dome, the reflecting pools that mirror its splendor, every facet is a brushstroke of architectural emotion.

Yet, it's the Taj's unique interplay with light that truly sets it apart. Watch as the sun's tender embrace transforms its marble surface from rose hues to luminescent white, as if echoing the many shades of love itself. This delicate dance between the structure and its surroundings imparts a profound lesson to architects and dreamers – that a building can breathe, evolve, and resonate with the world around it.

In its ivory embrace lies not just a monument, but a history lesson woven with threads of cultural exchange and creativity. The Taj Mahal stands as a testament to the craftsmanship of artisans and the visionary genius of architects who dared to bring to life a palace of pure love. Its influence echoes in the hearts of countless admirers and artists, inviting them to infuse their own creations with love and dedication.

As you stand before the Taj Mahal, let its story wash over you like a gentle monsoon rain. It is a tribute to the power of human passion, the pursuit of perfection, and the belief that love can transcend the confines of time and space. Architects and admirers alike, take heed – the Taj whispers that with devotion, creativity, and a touch of poetry, even the most extraordinary dreams can be carved from the unyielding stone of reality.

3

Eiffel Tower, France

Amidst the charming streets of Paris, a monumental iron marvel reaches skyward, capturing both the imagination and the heart of all who behold it – the Eiffel Tower. This iconic structure is not just a symbol of France, but a testament to the heights of human ingenuity and the artistry that can be woven from steel and dreams.

Imagine a time in the late 19th century when the world was on the cusp of a new era, teeming with the energy of progress and innovation. Gustave Eiffel, a visionary engineer, brought forth the Eiffel Tower for the 1889 World's Fair, a celebration of the industrial age. Little did he know that his creation would stand not only as a testament to his brilliance but as a beacon of human achievement for generations to come.

The Eiffel Tower's design whispers a story of ambition and modernity. Its iron lattice structure, a daring departure from the ornate architecture of its time, rises with elegance and strength. Each rivet, each beam, tells of a marriage between art and engineering – a melding of form and function that stirs the soul. It's as if the tower reaches not only for the sky but also into the hearts of those who dare to dream.

But perhaps its greatest magic lies in its philosophical resonance. As you gaze upon its intricate lattice, consider the tower's message – that even in a world of rapid change, there is beauty in embracing innovation. Just as the Eiffel Tower stood tall as a testament to progress, so too can we rise above challenges with grace and courage.

Time's tapestry weaves through the Eiffel Tower's girders, connecting us with the past, present, and future. It has stood witness to revolutions, artistic movements, and the dreams of millions who've climbed its heights. Architects and dreamers, take heed – the Eiffel Tower whispers that innovation knows no bounds, that daring to be different can result in structures that change the course of history.

As you stand beneath the Eiffel Tower's shadow, let its legacy embrace you. It is not just an emblem of France, but a testament to human imagination and the ability to shape the world around us. The tower beckons you to dream, to create, and to stand tall as a testament to the boundless heights the human spirit can reach, even when forged from iron and steeped in dreams.

4

Colosseum, Italy

In the heart of ancient Rome, a colossal amphitheater stands as a testament to the grandeur of a civilization that once ruled vast stretches of the world – the Colosseum. This iconic structure is not just a relic of the past; it's a living story etched in stone, a symbol of human ambition and the ceaseless thirst for entertainment, culture, and architectural innovation.

Imagine a time when the world was a tapestry of empires and conquests, and the city of Rome pulsated with life. The Colosseum, originally known as the Flavian Amphitheatre, emerged under the watchful gaze of emperors Vespasian and Titus in the 1st century AD. A magnificent arena, designed to host epic gladiatorial contests, wild animal hunts, and elaborate dramas, it captured the essence of Roman society – a blend of power, spectacle, and artistry.

The Colosseum's design is an ode to both functionality and symbolism. With its elliptical shape and tiered seating, it could accommodate a staggering 50,000 to 80,000 spectators. Beneath the surface, intricate systems of tunnels, ramps, and cages facilitated the mesmerizing spectacles. But beyond its engineering marvel, the Colosseum's design serves as a visual metaphor – a reflection of Rome's dominance and the unity of its people, gathered to experience the thrill of the arena.

As you stand before its arches and crumbling walls, imagine the echoes of history – the roars of the crowd, the clash of steel, and the stories etched into its very foundation. The Colosseum witnessed the splendor and savagery of ancient Roman life, a microcosm of a society driven by both valor and excess. It stands as a reminder that our architectural creations are not just physical structures; they are vessels that carry the collective memory of generations.

Architects and enthusiasts, heed the Colosseum's timeless message – that every design is a narrative, a reflection of the values and aspirations of its time. Just as the Colosseum symbolized Rome's ethos, so too can your creations encapsulate the spirit of your era and inspire those who come after you.

As you explore the Colosseum's corridors and corridors, let its whispers of the past ignite your imagination. It is more than just a ruin; it's a chapter in the ever-unfolding saga of humanity. The Colosseum beckons you to design not just for the present, but for the legacy you'll leave behind – a legacy that will echo through time, just as the grandeur of Rome still resonates in the heart of the Colosseum.

5

Sydney Opera House, Australia

Nestled along the sun-kissed shores of Sydney Harbor, the Sydney Opera House stands as a symphony of architectural innovation and cultural resonance. This iconic masterpiece isn't just a building; it's a vessel that carries the spirit of Australia's artistic soul and the limitless possibilities of human imagination.

Imagine a time when the world was yearning for a new expression of creativity, a beacon of cultural identity that could inspire generations. The Sydney Opera House emerged from the visionary mind of Danish architect Jørn Utzon, whose design won an international competition in 1957. With its billowing sails and sculptural elegance, the Opera House heralded a new chapter in architectural history.

The Opera House's design is poetry in motion. Its soaring shells seem to dance against the backdrop of the azure sky and the gentle lapping of the harbor waters. These shells aren't just aesthetic marvels; they are the embodiment of Utzon's philosophy that architecture should embrace nature's forms, echoing the sea, the sky, and the sails of boats navigating the harbor.

As you gaze upon the Opera House's iconic silhouette, envision the collaboration between human ingenuity and nature's grace. Each precast concrete panel was meticulously crafted, embracing the art of innovation. The use of groundbreaking engineering techniques in the 1960s, such as the application of computer-aided design, made the construction of these unique shells possible. The Opera House whispers a lesson to architects and dreamers – that even the most audacious visions can be realized with unwavering determination and an embrace of innovation.

Yet, the Opera House's impact is not just in its design; it reverberates through the annals of history. It has become Australia's cultural icon, a hub for artistic expression that transcends borders and languages. Its stages have hosted world-class performers, thinkers, and visionaries, drawing audiences into a world where imagination knows no limits.

Architects and creators, take heed of the Opera House's call – that your designs can be more than just structures. They can be catalysts for cultural evolution, sources of inspiration that uplift societies and unite people under the banner of shared creativity.

As you stand before the Sydney Opera House's luminous shells, remember that its story is not just about architecture; it's about humanity's ability to craft dreams from the canvas of reality. Let its presence encourage you to think beyond the ordinary, to shape structures that not only defy gravity but elevate the human spirit. The Sydney Opera House isn't just an icon; it's a reminder that your designs can echo through time, leaving an indelible mark on the world's cultural tapestry.

6

Statue of Liberty, USA

Standing tall in the embrace of New York Harbor, the Statue of Liberty stands as a timeless sentinel of freedom and hope. This iconic figure isn't merely a sculpture; it's a universal symbol that embodies the resilience of the human spirit and the pursuit of liberty.

Imagine an era when the world was brimming with dreams of a better life, a time when immigrants set their sights on America's welcoming shores. The Statue of Liberty, a gift from the people of France to the United States in 1886, emerged as a beacon of friendship and democracy. Designed by Frédéric Auguste Bartholdi and engineered by Gustave Eiffel, this colossal figure was more than just copper and iron; it was a proclamation that liberty knows no bounds.

The Statue's design radiates both elegance and strength. Her flowing robes, crowned with a radiant diadem, exude grace and dignity, while her raised torch symbolizes enlightenment that guides ships through the darkness. At her feet lies a broken chain, a powerful reminder of freedom from oppression.

As you gaze upon her majestic form, imagine the hands that shaped her, the minds that conceived her, and the hearts that embraced her message. The Statue of Liberty reminds us that great endeavors require collaboration, creativity, and a belief in the power of unity.

But her influence is more than just physical; it's etched into the heart of history. For countless immigrants, the sight of Lady Liberty was a promise of a new beginning, a sanctuary from tyranny. Her inscription, "Give me your tired, your poor, your huddled masses yearning to breathe free," reverberates through time, reminding us that compassion and inclusion are the cornerstones of a vibrant society.

Let the Statue of Liberty's outstretched arm guide your thoughts toward the horizon of possibility. Architects, dreamers, and lovers of liberty – heed her call. Just as she illuminates the harbor, your creations can illuminate minds and ignite passions. The Statue whispers to us that in the face of challenges, freedom shines like a beacon, reminding us that our designs can be more than structures; they can be testaments to the enduring power of human aspiration.

7

Burj Khalifa, UAE

Amidst the shimmering desert sands of the United Arab Emirates, a colossal spire of ambition pierces the heavens – the Burj Khalifa. This iconic skyscraper isn't just a tower; it's a testament to the audacity of human vision and the boundless heights of architectural achievement.

Imagine a world where cities compete to touch the sky, where innovation and luxury intertwine. The Burj Khalifa emerged as the pinnacle of this pursuit, born from the dreams of Sheikh Mohammed bin Rashid Al Maktoum. Designed by Adrian Smith, this architectural masterpiece took shape against a backdrop of modernity and tradition, a tribute to Dubai's relentless pursuit of excellence.

The Burj Khalifa's design is a study in geometry and elegance. Its slender form rises like a needle, a marvel of structural engineering. Each tier tapers gracefully, culminating in a needle-like spire that pierces the clouds. Its facade is adorned with a rhythmic pattern of glass and steel, capturing the essence of Dubai's forward-thinking spirit.

As you stand beneath its towering stature, envision the intricate dance between artistry and technology that brought it to life. Innovative construction methods and cutting-edge materials allowed engineers to conquer gravity itself. The Burj Khalifa isn't just a building; it's a symphony of human ingenuity.

But its significance reaches far beyond its staggering height. The Burj Khalifa is a beacon of economic and cultural transformation, a testament to Dubai's meteoric rise from a desert town to a global hub. It stands as a metaphor for the UAE's journey of innovation, reminding us that with vision and perseverance, even the seemingly impossible becomes attainable.

Architects and dreamers, let the Burj Khalifa's towering form be a reminder of the heights you can scale. Just as its spire brushes against the heavens, so too can your creations touch the realms of imagination. The Burj Khalifa beckons us to dream big, to believe that our designs can shape not only skylines but the very fabric of history.

As you gaze up at the Burj Khalifa's gleaming façade, remember that it's not just a tower; it's a testament to humanity's unyielding pursuit of greatness.

Let it inspire you to craft designs that defy limits and challenge norms, for just as Dubai transformed its skyline, your creations can transform the world.

8

Parthenon, Greece

Nestled atop the Athenian Acropolis, a timeless marvel rises against the backdrop of a rich historical tapestry – the Parthenon. This iconic temple isn't just a structure; it's a whisper of ancient wisdom, a testament to the enduring pursuit of beauty and the indomitable spirit of a civilization that laid the foundations of democracy.

Imagine an era when Greece was a crucible of ideas, a land where philosophy, art, and governance intertwined. The Parthenon emerged during the Golden Age of Athens, a tribute to the goddess Athena. Designed by architects Ictinus and Callicrates, this symmetrical marvel wasn't just a temple; it was a monument to ideals and excellence.

The Parthenon's design speaks of harmony and proportion, a reflection of Greece's philosophical exploration of balance and aesthetics. Its columns stand as graceful testaments to the Doric order, a celebration of simplicity and symmetry. The temple's slight curvature and subtleties counteract optical illusions, demonstrating the architects' acute understanding of geometry.

As you envision yourself standing before this ancient marvel, the ghosts of history whisper tales of its construction. Imagine the skilled artisans chiseling away, shaping the marble blocks that would create a legacy. The Parthenon isn't just a building; it's a hymn to human craftsmanship.

But its significance doesn't merely rest in its form; it's etched into the annals of history. The Parthenon bore witness to the birth of democracy, standing as a symbol of Athens' flourishing cultural and political achievements. It embodies the ideals of a society that celebrated art, reason, and the quest for knowledge.

Architects and thinkers, allow the Parthenon's columns to be your pillars of inspiration. Just as its design reflects the pursuit of perfection, so too can your creations echo the spirit of excellence. The Parthenon teaches us that great ideas are timeless, that craftsmanship leaves an indelible mark across the ages.

As you peer upon the Parthenon's majestic ruins, remember that it's more than just an ancient structure; it's a bridge to a world where humanity's quest for truth and beauty was etched in stone. Let its legacy inspire you to design not just for the present, but for the generations yet to come – for just as the Parthenon stands resilient, your creations can stand as echoes of greatness in the vast symphony of history.

9

Machu Picchu, Peru

In the heart of the Andes mountains, a mystical city whispers its secrets to the winds – Machu Picchu. This enigmatic citadel isn't just a collection of stone structures; it's a portal to a forgotten world, a testament to the intricate harmony between human ingenuity and the raw beauty of nature.

Imagine a time when the Inca civilization thrived in the rugged terrain of Peru, their wisdom interwoven with the landscape. Machu Picchu was built around the 15th century, perched upon a mountain ridge that seems to touch the heavens. Designed with the cosmos in mind, this city wasn't just a fortress; it was a spiritual haven, a place of pilgrimage and veneration.

Machu Picchu's design is a marvel of engineering that defies the elements. The precision with which its stones were fitted, without mortar, speaks to the Inca's mastery of construction. Its terraced fields, intricate stone walls, and ceremonial spaces meld seamlessly into the mountainscape, as if nature herself collaborated in its creation.

As you conjure an image of this ancient wonder, envision the lives that once flourished within its stone embrace. The Incas designed Machu Picchu to harmonize with the solstices and equinoxes, a testament to their profound connection to the cosmos. The city isn't just a relic; it's a memory of a civilization that understood the interplay between the earthly and the celestial.

Yet, its relevance extends beyond its architectural brilliance. Machu Picchu symbolizes the resilience of the human spirit and the passage of time. Abandoned and concealed by nature for centuries, it was rediscovered in 1911 by Hiram Bingham, sparking worldwide fascination and igniting curiosity about the ancient world.

Architects and adventurers, heed Machu Picchu's silent whispers. Just as the Incas harmonized with nature, so too can your designs evoke a sense of unity with the environment. The citadel beckons us to remember that our creations are not just structures; they are conduits that can transport us through history and evoke a deep sense of wonder.

As you contemplate the majesty of Machu Picchu's ruins, remember that it's more than just a city; it's a journey through time, a fragment of a story that spans centuries. Let its legacy inspire you to design with a reverence for nature and an understanding that your creations can leave imprints not just on landscapes, but on the very soul of humanity.

10

Saint Basil's Cathedral, Russia

Amid the mystique of Moscow's Red Square, a kaleidoscope of colors and curves reaches for the heavens – Saint Basil's Cathedral. This iconic masterpiece isn't just a cathedral; it's a symphony of whimsy, a testament to the exuberance of faith and the boundless imagination of architectural brilliance.

Imagine a time when Russia's history was as intricate as its onion domes, and Ivan the Terrible's reign was both turbulent and transformative. Saint Basil's Cathedral emerged in the 16th century as a tribute to Ivan's victory over the Khanate of Kazan. Its design, often attributed to the architect Postnik Yakovlev, defies the conventions of religious architecture, inviting awe and wonder.

Saint Basil's design is a mosaic of hues and forms, each dome resembling an onion, a flame, or a precious gem. Its radiant colors dance in the sunlight, echoing the festive spirit of Moscow's celebrations. This cathedral isn't just a place of worship; it's a celebration of faith, a canvas painted with devotion and imagination.

As you envision yourself strolling through the heart of Red Square, picture the artisans who crafted this dreamlike realm. Their hands shaped the bricks and tiles that would become a testament to human creativity. Saint Basil's isn't just a building; it's a testament to the audacity of architectural vision.

Yet, its influence is more than just aesthetic; it's intertwined with the tale of Russia's history. Saint Basil's Cathedral bears witness to the country's triumphs and tribulations, a resilient figure that's stood against the backdrop of czars, revolutions, and the march of time. It encapsulates Russia's spiritual fervor and the intertwining of faith and culture.

Architects and dreamers, let Saint Basil's Cathedral's whimsical domes inspire your own flights of imagination. Just as its design transcends norms, so too can your creations stretch the boundaries of convention. The cathedral reminds us that beauty can be both sacred and spectacular.

As you stand before Saint Basil's Cathedral's radiant façade, remember that it's not just a collection of domes; it's a testament to the vibrancy of faith and the limitless potential of creativity. Let its legacy encourage you to design with abandon, to embrace the unconventional, and to let your architectural visions bloom like the radiant petals of an eternal spring.

11

Sagrada Família, Spain

In the heart of Barcelona, a symphony of stone soars toward the heavens – the Sagrada Família. This iconic basilica isn't merely a building; it's a living, breathing poem etched in stone, a testament to the indomitable spirit of a visionary architect and the transcendence of human creativity.

Imagine a world where architecture becomes an embodiment of spirituality, where faith takes form in marble and light. The Sagrada Família was conceived by the brilliant Antoni Gaudí, his vision and design flowing from a deep wellspring of inspiration. The basilica's construction began in 1882 and continues to this day, a testament to the dedication of countless artisans, architects, and dreamers.

The Sagrada Família's design is a symphony of symbolism and innovation. Its towering spires and intricate facades weave stories of the Bible and the essence of creation. The columns branch out like trees, supporting the roof in an organic dance of stone. Its stained glass windows flood the interior with a kaleidoscope of colors, illuminating a sacred space that transcends the boundaries of time and matter.

As you imagine standing before this cathedral of dreams, envision the artisans who sculpted its stone, the architects who breathed life into its blueprints. The Sagrada Família isn't just a structure; it's an ode to dedication and human ingenuity.

Yet, its significance reaches far beyond the beauty of its forms. The Sagrada Família stands as a tribute to Gaudí's belief that architecture could mirror the very soul of humanity. It's a reminder that dreams are woven into the very fabric of history, that creativity can defy the constraints of time.

Architects and visionaries, let the Sagrada Família's soaring spires guide your aspirations. Just as Gaudí's designs melded nature and spirituality, so too can your creations blend the worlds of the tangible and the ethereal. The basilica whispers that every line you draw, every detail you conceive, can be a brushstroke on the canvas of human expression.

As you contemplate the majesty of the Sagrada Família's forms, remember that it's more than just a basilica; it's a journey of human dedication and the fusion of art and faith. Let its legacy inspire you to design not merely for the present, but for the generations that will follow – for just as Gaudí sculpted his dreams in stone, your creations can shape the world's skyline and stir the soul of humanity.

12

Forbidden City, China

Nestled at the heart of Beijing, a majestic fortress unfolds like a reverie of ancient dynasties – the Forbidden City. This iconic palace complex isn't just a collection of buildings; it's a living chapter in China's history, an architectural ode to power and cultural legacy.

Picture an era when emperors held court in a world veiled in mystery and grandeur. The Forbidden City was constructed in the early 15th century during the Ming Dynasty, a sprawling testament to the might of Chinese imperial rule. For centuries, its towering gates and opulent halls hosted emperors, eunuchs, and concubines, shrouded in an air of exclusivity and power.

The Forbidden City's design is a dance between art and symbolism. Its meticulous layout aligns with ancient principles of harmony and balance. The complex consists of precisely arranged courtyards, palaces, and halls that flow seamlessly like a river of history. Each element, from the imperial yellow rooftops to the intricate carvings, carries the weight of tradition and philosophy.

As you visualize walking through its imposing gates, picture the artisans and laborers who transformed visions into stone. The Forbidden City isn't just a palace; it's a manifestation of human ambition, a reflection of the unyielding spirit that drove generations to shape a legacy.

However, its significance spans beyond its architecture. The Forbidden City witnessed China's rise and transformation, its cultural evolution and the passage of dynasties. It's a silent witness to the narratives of emperors and the pulse of a nation that stretches beyond its walls.

Architects and dreamers, let the Forbidden City's intricate design inspire your own creative endeavors. Just as its layout reflects ancient philosophies, so too can your creations embody the spirit of cultures and the wisdom of the ages. The palace complex whispers that every stone and corridor can be a repository of stories and a bridge to history.

As you ponder the vastness of the Forbidden City's halls, remember that it's more than just architecture; it's a symphony of human achievement, a canvas painted with the hues of power, culture, and time. Let its legacy motivate you to design spaces that don't just shelter lives, but tell tales, shape identities, and carve niches in the annals of history.

13

Angkor Wat, Cambodia

Amidst the lush jungles of Cambodia, a testament to human ingenuity and spiritual devotion emerges – Angkor Wat. This iconic temple complex isn't just a collection of ruins; it's a living reverie of ancient civilizations, a symphony of stone that resonates with the echoes of history and the whispers of ancient gods.

Imagine a time when empires flourished in the heart of Southeast Asia, and Cambodia's landscape bore witness to a flourishing civilization. Angkor Wat was constructed in the 12th century by King Suryavarman II, a visionary ruler who sought to create a temple that bridged the realms of heaven and earth. This architectural marvel is more than just a temple; it's a hymn to the divine, a canvas that tells the stories of gods and mortals.

Angkor Wat's design transcends mere architecture; it's a philosophical journey carved in stone. Its intricate layout reflects the Hindu cosmology, with the towering central spire symbolizing Mount Meru, the mythical abode of gods. The complex's intricate bas-reliefs chronicle tales from epics and depict life in the Khmer Empire with remarkable detail, bridging the gap between history and spirituality.

As you picture yourself wandering through the temple's halls, imagine the hands that chiseled each intricate detail, the artists who painted stories on its walls. Angkor Wat isn't just a ruin; it's a testament to human craftsmanship and the indomitable spirit that shaped civilizations.

Yet, its influence reaches far beyond its time. Angkor Wat embodies the grandeur of a bygone era, reminding us of the cultural tapestry that once adorned Cambodia. It's a testimony to the resilience of human achievements and a mirror reflecting the cycles of life, from the zenith of empires to the quiet embrace of nature.

Architects and dreamers, let Angkor Wat's intricate beauty inspire your own visions. Just as its design merges heaven and earth, so too can your creations blend innovation with reverence. The temple complex whispers that every arch and carving can hold the stories of generations and the essence of a culture.

ANGKOR WAT, CAMBODIA

As you envision the sun rising over Angkor Wat's spires, remember that it's not just a temple; it's a bridge that connects us to history, spirituality, and the marvels of human creation. Let its legacy encourage you to design not just for today, but for the generations to come – for just as Angkor Wat still stands, your creations can be an echo of greatness across the sands of time.

14

Westminster Abbey, UK

Amidst the heart of London, where history's whispers intertwine with the present, stands a living tapestry of heritage and faith – Westminster Abbey. This iconic abbey isn't merely a building; it's a sanctuary where the pages of history are etched in stone, a symphony of architecture that echoes the journey of a nation and the threads that weave humanity together.

Imagine an era when kings and queens forged destinies and poets penned verses that traversed time. Westminster Abbey's origins trace back to the 7th century, a place of worship that evolved into a site of coronations, weddings, and final rest for luminaries. Its hallowed walls have borne witness to the annals of British history and the pulse of a nation's soul.

Westminster Abbey's design isn't just an arrangement of stone; it's a homage to continuity and transcendence. The abbey's Gothic architecture reaches skyward, its intricate arches and soaring spires reminiscent of nature's grandeur. Its chapels, nave, and transepts form a spiritual labyrinth that echoes with the whispers of saints, rulers, and artists.

As you visualize walking through its hallowed halls, envision the architects and craftsmen who labored through the centuries. Westminster Abbey isn't just a structure; it's a testament to human perseverance and the sanctity of creation.

Yet, its significance stretches far beyond its walls. Westminster Abbey is more than a place of worship; it's a mirror reflecting the tapestry of British history. It's the place where monarchs have been crowned and statesmen laid to rest. It's where literary giants like Shakespeare and Dickens found eternal repose. It's a sanctuary where the threads of the past continue to influence the tapestry of the present.

Architects and dreamers, let Westminster Abbey's time-worn stones inspire your own creative journey. Just as its architecture bridges eras, so too can your designs fuse innovation with reverence for tradition. The abbey beckons us to remember that every line you sketch, every detail you shape, can be a bridge between history and tomorrow.

As you contemplate the majesty of Westminster Abbey's arches, remember that it's more than just a building; it's a testament to humanity's quest for meaning and legacy. Let its legacy guide you to design not just for the moment, but for the echoes that will reverberate through time – for just as Westminster Abbey has stood as a sentinel of history, so too can your creations stand as guardians of innovation and tradition in the grand journey of existence.

15

Petra, Jordan

Nestled within the rose-red embrace of the Jordanian desert, a city carved from the very heart of stone beckons with its ancient allure – Petra. This iconic archaeological wonder isn't just a collection of ruins; it's a testament to the tenacity of human spirit, a symphony of ingenuity harmonizing with nature's grandeur.

Imagine a time when civilizations thrived in the arid lands of the Middle East, and Petra emerged as a bustling hub of trade and culture. Founded around the 4th century BC, this rose-red city was the capital of the Nabatean Kingdom, a people who hewed their homes, tombs, and temples from the very cliffs that sheltered them. Petra is more than just a city; it's a testament to human adaptability and harmonious coexistence with the environment.

Petra's design isn't just architecture; it's a masterpiece of nature and human craft intertwined. The narrow, sinuous Siq – a gorge carved by water and time – serves as a portal, revealing the Treasury with breathtaking drama. This monumental structure stands as a greeting from the ancients, a welcome etched in stone. Its intricate facades blend Hellenistic and Eastern influences, a testament to the crossroads of cultures that found sanctuary within Petra's sandstone embrace.

As you visualize yourself wandering through the Siq and gazing at the Treasury, picture the hands that carved the intricate details and shaped the stones. Petra isn't just a collection of structures; it's a symphony of determination, a testament to the human ability to transform the unforgiving into the extraordinary.

Yet, its significance reaches far beyond its ancient origins. Petra has stood as a crossroads of empires and cultures, a melting pot where caravans and ideas converged. Its history is a living mosaic of Nabatean, Roman, and Byzantine influences. It's a testament to the importance of trade and the transcendent power of unity amidst diversity.

Architects and explorers, let Petra's monumental grandeur inspire your own creative endeavors. Just as its structures meld with nature, so too can your designs embrace the environment while celebrating human artistry. Petra whispers that every stone you place can carry the stories of millennia and become a bridge to the past.

As you conjure the hues of Petra's rose-red cliffs, remember that it's more than just an archaeological site; it's a testament to human resilience, a canvas painted with the pigments of civilizations long past. Let its legacy remind you to design not just for the now, but for the echoes that will resonate across generations – for just as Petra's sandstone walls stand as a testament to history's whispers, so too can your creations become guardians of culture and innovation through the sands of time.

16

Christ the Redeemer, Brazil

At the summit of Corcovado Mountain, a monumental figure of grace and serenity stretches its arms wide – Christ the Redeemer. This iconic statue isn't just a sculpture; it's a beacon of hope that transcends boundaries, an embodiment of faith and the universal embrace of humanity.

Imagine a world where spirituality finds expression in stone and steel, and Rio de Janeiro becomes the canvas for a transcendent message. Christ the Redeemer was unveiled in 1931, a gift from Brazil to the world, a testament to faith and unity. The statue stands as a towering guardian, overlooking the city below with an air of serenity.

Christ the Redeemer's design isn't just an arrangement of materials; it's a symphony of purpose and philosophy. Its open arms evoke a sense of welcome, a gesture of peace that bridges cultures and creeds. The statue's Art Deco style and its harmonious integration with the surrounding landscape make it a testament to the convergence of art, nature, and spirituality.

As you imagine standing before the statue's imposing presence, visualize the hands that sculpted its form, the minds that conceived its proportions. Christ the Redeemer isn't just a statue; it's a manifestation of human devotion, a tribute to the heights we can reach when inspired by faith.

Yet, its influence spans far beyond its physicality. Christ the Redeemer stands not just as a symbol of Christianity, but as a symbol of hope, compassion, and unity. It has become a global icon, drawing pilgrims, tourists, and seekers of inspiration. It's a reminder that even in a diverse world, there are shared values that connect us all.

Dreamers and believers, let Christ the Redeemer's embrace guide your creative aspirations. Just as its arms stretch wide, so too can your designs reach across boundaries and cultures, fostering connections that transcend differences. The statue whispers that every stroke of creativity can become a bridge between hearts and souls.

As you contemplate the majesty of Christ the Redeemer's silhouette against the sky, remember that it's more than just a statue; it's a testament to the power of belief and the potential of human collaboration. Let its legacy remind you to design not just for structures, but for the emotions they can evoke and the connections they can foster. For just as Christ the Redeemer's arms embrace the world, so too can your creations become beacons of inspiration, uniting hearts across the vast canvas of existence.

17

Leaning Tower of Pisa, Italy

In the charming embrace of Pisa, Italy, a tower with a heartwarming tilt stands as a testament to the whimsy of architecture and the unpredictability of human creation – the Leaning Tower of Pisa. This iconic tower isn't just a slanted structure; it's a global smile, a lighthearted reminder that even in the face of unintended twists, beauty and history flourish.

Imagine a time when medieval Italy was a canvas for grand artistic endeavors. The Leaning Tower of Pisa's journey began in the 12th century as a free-standing bell tower, an accompaniment to the nearby cathedral. The tower's distinctive tilt wasn't planned; it resulted from the soft subsoil of the site, lending it a playful and endearing slant.

The Leaning Tower of Pisa's design isn't just architecture; it's a dance between stability and serendipity. Its white marble façade, adorned with arches and columns, exudes elegance, a delicate touch that defies its eccentric lean. Its seven levels spiral toward the sky, with each floor a canvas for masterful craftsmanship.

As you imagine yourself standing before this tilted wonder, picture the artisans who shaped its marbled exterior and the architects who navigated the tower's unexpected twist. The Leaning Tower of Pisa isn't just a tower; it's a testament to the creative ways humans adapt to challenges and turn them into marvels.

Yet, its significance stretches far beyond its slant. The tower's lean isn't just a peculiarity; it's a symbol of resilience and human innovation. It has become an emblem of Pisa's unique charm and a worldwide icon of human triumph over the whims of fate.

Dreamers and creators, let the Leaning Tower of Pisa's whimsicality guide your artistic endeavors. Just as its tilt became its signature, so too can your designs embrace the unexpected and turn it into a mark of distinction. The tower's story whispers that every imperfection can be an opportunity for creativity to shine.

As you ponder the Leaning Tower of Pisa's off-kilter beauty, remember that it's more than just a tilted tower; it's a lesson in embracing the twists and turns of life with grace and ingenuity. Let its legacy inspire you to design not just for perfection, but for the journey – for just as the tower's slant endears it to the world, so too can your creations win hearts with their authenticity and the spirit of adaptation.

18

Neuschwanstein Castle, Germany

Amidst the enchanting landscapes of Germany, a fairytale castle rises like a dream from the pages of a storybook – Neuschwanstein Castle. This iconic fortress isn't just a castle; it's a symphony of imagination and romanticism, a testament to the power of dreams and the enduring allure of architectural fantasy.

NEUSCHWANSTEIN CASTLE, GERMANY

Imagine a time when kings were visionaries and castles weren't just fortifications, but reflections of the human spirit. Neuschwanstein Castle emerged in the 19th century, a brainchild of King Ludwig II of Bavaria. With a heart yearning for the romantic past and an eye for the fantastical, he sought to create a castle that blended medieval charm with whimsical grandeur.

Neuschwanstein Castle's design isn't just architecture; it's an embodiment of imagination's boundless frontiers. Its soaring turrets, delicate spires, and artistic flourishes evoke the enchantment of fairy tales. The castle's pristine white walls rise against the backdrop of the Bavarian Alps, mirroring the fantasies that inspired its creation.

As you picture yourself wandering through the castle's lavish chambers, envision the artisans and craftsmen who brought Ludwig's vision to life. Neuschwanstein Castle isn't just a structure; it's a testament to the artistry that springs forth from the depths of the human soul.

Yet, its significance extends beyond its aesthetic splendor. Neuschwanstein Castle isn't merely a royal residence; it's a symbol of Ludwig's love for art and music, a sanctuary where he retreated from the complexities of monarchy to immerse himself in his creative passions. It's a touchstone of the Romantic movement, reflecting the yearning for a simpler, more wondrous world.

Dreamers and creators, let Neuschwanstein Castle's whimsy guide your artistic endeavors. Just as its design marries reality with the realm of dreams, so too can your creations blend the tangible with the imaginative. The castle's story whispers that every corner you carve, every detail you shape, can be an echo of your soul's yearnings.

As you contemplate Neuschwanstein Castle's ethereal beauty against the alpine backdrop, remember that it's more than just a castle; it's an ode to human aspiration and the magic of creativity. Let its legacy encourage you to design not just for functionality, but for the enchantment that can lift spirits and awaken the dreamer in us all. For just as Neuschwanstein Castle stands as a testament to Ludwig's reverie, so too can your creations weave a tapestry of wonder that resonates through time.

19

Alhambra, Spain

In the heart of Granada, Spain, a palatial masterpiece emerges like a vision from tales of a distant era – the Alhambra. This iconic complex isn't just a collection of walls; it's a symphony of Moorish artistry, an intricate tapestry that weaves together the threads of history, culture, and architectural brilliance.

Imagine a time when the Iberian Peninsula resonated with the harmony of diverse cultures. The Alhambra was born in the 13th century, a testament to the Nasrid dynasty's legacy and their passion for creating an earthly paradise. This palace and fortress complex stands as a testament to the Moorish dynasty's love for poetry, gardens, and architectural beauty.

The Alhambra's design isn't just architecture; it's an eloquent expression of philosophy. Its intricate courtyards, intricate geometric patterns, and arabesque motifs speak of a deep connection between nature and spirituality. The Generalife gardens within the complex, with their serene pools and lush flora, reflect the Moors' reverence for harmony and the transcendence of earthly concerns.

As you envision yourself strolling through the Alhambra's stunning halls, picture the skilled craftsmen who chiseled delicate details into the stone and the artisans who painted the intricate tiles. The Alhambra isn't just a monument; it's a testament to the hands that shaped it and the stories it holds.

Yet, its influence stretches far beyond its walls. The Alhambra is more than a palace; it's a testament to the interplay of cultures and the transcendent power of art and architecture. It's a UNESCO World Heritage Site that encapsulates centuries of history, from the Moors to the Catholic Monarchs, speaking of a time when civilizations converged and flourished.

Dreamers and creators, let the Alhambra's intricate beauty guide your artistic endeavors. Just as its designs blend art with nature, so too can your creations merge innovation with reverence for heritage. The complex's story whispers that every stroke of creativity can echo through time and become a testament to the human pursuit of beauty and harmony.

As you contemplate the Alhambra's graceful arches against the backdrop of the Sierra Nevada mountains, remember that it's more than just a palace;

it's a living reminder of the synthesis of cultures, the power of creativity, and the timeless quest for unity. Let its legacy inspire you to design not just for the moment, but for the echoes that will resonate through generations – for just as the Alhambra's walls hold history's whispers, so too can your creations become vessels of culture and innovation, transcending time's boundaries.

20

Hagia Sophia, Turkey

Amid the captivating cityscape of Istanbul, a timeless wonder rises with an air of grandeur – the Hagia Sophia. This iconic structure isn't just a building; it's a symphony of spirituality and architectural brilliance that spans empires and epochs, a testament to the enduring pursuit of beauty and knowledge.

Imagine a world where Byzantium thrived as a crossroads of culture, and the Hagia Sophia emerged as a marvel of the Byzantine Empire. Originally built in the 6th century as a cathedral, it stood as a beacon of Christianity's luminance. Then, with the ebb and flow of history's tides, it was transformed into a mosque in the 15th century, and finally, into a museum in the 20th century. The Hagia Sophia's story isn't just about one era; it's a saga that mirrors the metamorphosis of a city and the spirit of its inhabitants.

The Hagia Sophia's design isn't just architecture; it's a dialogue between the celestial and the earthly. Its vast dome, supported by massive piers and punctuated by windows that appear to float, creates an illusion of levitation, a harmonious interplay between light and space. Its interior is adorned with intricate mosaics that recount stories of faith and humanity's yearning for transcendence.

As you picture yourself walking through the Hagia Sophia's majestic halls, envision the architects who dared to dream of such a marvel and the artisans who turned their visions into stone and mosaic. The Hagia Sophia isn't just a structure; it's a testament to the boundless potential of human hands guided by vision and dedication.

Yet, its significance extends far beyond its architecture. The Hagia Sophia stands not only as a religious and cultural symbol, but as a bridge that unites empires and belief systems. It has witnessed the rise and fall of dynasties, the merging of cultures, and the metamorphosis of Istanbul from Byzantium to Constantinople to the vibrant metropolis it is today.

Dreamers and creators, let the Hagia Sophia's celestial elegance inspire your artistic pursuits. Just as its design melds sacred and secular, so too can your creations embody the unity of diverse influences. The Hagia Sophia's tale whispers that every stroke of your imagination can be a brushstroke on the canvas of history.

As you contemplate the Hagia Sophia's majestic dome against the city's skyline, remember that it's more than just a monument; it's a testament to the confluence of faith, art, and human endeavor. Let its legacy embolden you to design not just for today, but for the echoes that will reverberate across generations – for just as the Hagia Sophia's arches span centuries, so too can your creations transcend time, touching hearts and inspiring minds for ages to come.

21

Louvre Museum, France

Nestled along the Seine River in the heart of Paris, an artful fortress of culture and history unfolds its magnificent wings – the Louvre Museum. This iconic structure isn't just a museum; it's a time capsule of human creativity, a repository of treasures that whisper tales of civilizations past and inspire the dreams of generations to come.

Imagine a world where art is safeguarded like precious gems, and history is etched in brushstrokes and sculptures. The Louvre's story began centuries ago, once a royal palace and then transformed into a grand museum in the 18th century, opening its doors to the public's hungry curiosity. The Louvre isn't just a building; it's a guardian of artistic legacies, a symphony of culture that resonates through time.

The Louvre's design isn't just architecture; it's a dialogue between the old and the new, a dance of classicism and modernity. Its historic façade, with its intricate details and elegant arches, mirrors the grace of France's past. The pyramid at its entrance, a masterpiece of glass and steel, symbolizes the boldness of progress while honoring tradition.

As you picture yourself wandering through the Louvre's grand galleries, imagine the masterpieces that line its walls, the sculptures that adorn its halls. The Louvre isn't just a museum; it's a sanctuary for artistic brilliance and a testament to the visionaries who shaped the world with their creations.

Yet, its significance stretches far beyond its artful walls. The Louvre stands not just as a museum, but as a global icon of culture and knowledge. It houses the Mona Lisa's enigmatic smile, the timeless beauty of the Venus de Milo, and countless other treasures that transcend national boundaries, weaving together the stories of humanity.

Dreamers and admirers of beauty, let the Louvre's boundless creativity guide your own artistic endeavors. Just as its galleries house diverse styles and epochs, so too can your creations blend the old and the new, celebrating heritage while embracing innovation. The Louvre's legacy whispers that every stroke of your brush, every piece of your puzzle, can become part of the grand mosaic of human expression.

As you contemplate the Louvre's majestic façade under the Parisian sky, remember that it's more than just a museum; it's a celebration of the human spirit's yearning for creation and understanding. Let its legacy inspire you to design not just for aesthetics, but for the spark of curiosity and the illumination of minds – for just as the Louvre's halls echo with history's whispers, so too can your creations resonate through time, kindling passions and connecting souls in the grand tapestry of existence.

22

Potala Palace, Tibet

Amidst the majestic Himalayan peaks and the spiritual embrace of Tibet, a palace that reaches for the heavens stands as a testament to faith and earthly grandeur – the Potala Palace. This iconic structure isn't just a palace; it's a manifestation of devotion, an architectural marvel that blends the sacred with the sublime.

Imagine a realm where spirituality is woven into every thread of existence, and the Potala Palace emerges as a beacon of Tibetan Buddhism. Constructed in the 17th century, this palace was more than just the winter residence of the Dalai Lama; it was a sanctuary of wisdom and contemplation. The Potala Palace isn't just a building; it's a testament to the unity of faith and the heights humans can reach when they're guided by their beliefs.

The Potala Palace's design isn't just architecture; it's a journey of ascension, a prayer in stone and wood. Its white and red façade ascends along Marpo Ri, the Red Hill, as if seeking to touch the heavens. The intricate murals, delicate frescoes, and golden stupas that adorn its halls celebrate both earthly beauty and the spiritual quest.

As you imagine yourself climbing the palace's steps and entering its hallowed chambers, envision the monks who once tread these halls, the artisans who painted its stories. The Potala Palace isn't just a palace; it's a canvas of devotion, a symphony of the sacred and the artistic.

Yet, its significance spans far beyond its physical presence. The Potala Palace isn't just a structure; it's a touchstone of Tibetan identity and a symbol of the struggle for spiritual and cultural preservation. It has witnessed the flow of time, the tumultuous tides of history, and the resilience of a people bound to their beliefs.

Dreamers and seekers of truth, let the Potala Palace's spiritual grandeur guide your own aspirations. Just as its design bridges the earthly and the divine, so too can your creations embody the harmony of the soul's journey. The palace's story whispers that every stroke of your inspiration can become a brushstroke on the canvas of the cosmos.

As you contemplate the Potala Palace's towering silhouette against the Tibetan sky, remember that it's more than just a palace; it's a shrine to the human spirit's quest for meaning and enlightenment. Let its legacy inspire you to design not just for beauty, but for the elevation of the soul and the kindling of inner light – for just as the Potala Palace's spires touch the sky, so too can your creations transcend the ordinary, stirring hearts and evoking the sacred in the grand tapestry of existence.

23

Chichen Itza, Mexico

Amidst the lush jungles of the Yucatan Peninsula, a city frozen in time rises from the earth with mystique and magnificence – Chichen Itza. This iconic archaeological site isn't just a collection of ruins; it's a testament to the brilliance of ancient civilizations, a symphony of architecture and astronomy that bridges the gap between earth and sky.

Imagine a world where the Maya people gazed at the heavens with reverence, and Chichen Itza emerged as a cosmic masterpiece. Founded in the 6th century, this city was more than just a settlement; it was a cultural and ceremonial center. Chichen Itza isn't just a collection of stone; it's an archaeological treasure trove that holds the secrets of a civilization's intellect and spirituality.

Chichen Itza's design isn't just architecture; it's an ode to the cosmos, an architectural expression of the Maya's connection to the universe. The Pyramid of Kukulkan, also known as El Castillo, stands as a celestial calendar, with its 91 steps on each of its four sides totaling 364, plus the platform, symbolizing the 365 days of the solar year. On the spring and autumn equinoxes, the sunlight and shadows combine to create an illusion of a serpent slithering down the pyramid – a tribute to both architectural prowess and cosmic understanding.

As you picture yourself wandering through the ancient city's remnants, imagine the builders who meticulously placed each stone, the astronomers who mapped the stars. Chichen Itza isn't just a historical site; it's a living testament to human curiosity and the urge to uncover the mysteries of existence.

Yet, its significance reaches far beyond its time. Chichen Itza isn't just a relic; it's a UNESCO World Heritage Site that speaks of the ingenuity of the Maya civilization. It's a bridge between cultures, a symbol of the Maya's ability to merge architecture, mathematics, and spirituality into a harmonious whole.

Dreamers and explorers of knowledge, let Chichen Itza's celestial marvels inspire your own quests. Just as its design fuses sky and earth, so too can your creations marry innovation with reverence for the cosmos. Chichen Itza's story whispers that every question you ask, every discovery you make, can lead to a deeper connection with the universe.

As you contemplate the Pyramid of Kukulkan against the Yucatan's verdant landscape, remember that Chichen Itza is more than just a historical site; it's a journey through time, a testament to human intellect, and a reminder that the cosmos and the human spirit are forever intertwined. Let its legacy guide you to design not just for the present, but for the enigmatic journey of exploration and understanding – for just as Chichen Itza's stones echo with the wisdom of the ages, so too can your creations echo with the wonder of discovery, resonating through the annals of time.

24

Brandenburg Gate, Germany

Amidst the bustling heart of Berlin, a triumphant archway emerges as a testament to unity, freedom, and the indomitable spirit of a nation – the Brandenburg Gate. This iconic structure isn't just an arch; it's a symbol of history's twists and turns, a reminder that even in the face of division, humanity can bridge gaps and build bridges of hope.

Imagine a world where empires rose and fell, and the Brandenburg Gate stood as a sentinel between the past and the future. Constructed in the late 18th century, this monumental arch was more than just an entryway; it was a gateway to transformation. The Brandenburg Gate isn't just a structure; it's a portal to resilience, a beacon of light amidst history's shadows.

The Brandenburg Gate's design isn't just architecture; it's a testament to the endurance of ideals and the power of architecture to tell stories. Its six majestic columns rise to a chariot, crowned by the goddess Victoria, her triumphant stance echoing the aspirations of a nation. The gate's sandstone façade whispers of neoclassical elegance, a nod to the classical past while embracing the contemporary.

As you picture yourself passing through the Brandenburg Gate's towering columns, imagine the hands that shaped its stones, the minds that conceptualized its design. The Brandenburg Gate isn't just an arch; it's a reminder that even in the face of adversity, humanity's creative spirit can endure and flourish.

Yet, its significance spans far beyond its physical structure. The Brandenburg Gate isn't just an arch; it's a symbol of unity, a witness to history's sweeping changes. From the Prussian monarchy to the tumultuous days of World War II, from the Cold War divide to the joyful reunification of East and West Germany, the gate has stood as a silent witness to the turning tides of human destiny.

Dreamers and advocates of progress, let the Brandenburg Gate's archway of unity guide your creative endeavors. Just as its columns join together, so too can your creations celebrate the convergence of ideas and cultures. The gate's story whispers that every endeavor you embark upon, every project you nurture, can contribute to the tapestry of shared human experience.

As you contemplate the Brandenburg Gate's resplendent silhouette against

Berlin's vibrant backdrop, remember that it's more than just an arch; it's a testament to the unbreakable spirit of a nation and the transformative power of collective dreams. Let its legacy inspire you to design not just for aesthetics, but for the bonds that connect hearts and the aspirations that kindle change – for just as the Brandenburg Gate's columns stand united, so too can your creations be bridges that span divides and illuminate the path toward unity and progress.

25

Tower Bridge, UK

Amid the timeless elegance of London's skyline and the flowing embrace of the River Thames, a marvel of engineering and artistry stands as a symbol of connection and progress – the Tower Bridge. This iconic structure isn't just a bridge; it's a testament to innovation, a tribute to the human spirit's ability to bridge divides and span eras with grace and ingenuity.

Imagine a world where the industrial revolution ushered in a new era, and the Tower Bridge emerged as a masterpiece of Victorian engineering. Completed in the late 19th century, this bridge wasn't just a passage; it was a link between history and modernity. The Tower Bridge isn't just a structure; it's a testament to the confluence of art and mechanics, where form marries function.

The Tower Bridge's design isn't just architecture; it's a dance of steel and stone, a symphony of Victorian grandeur. Its twin bascules, or drawbridges, rise like monumental arms to allow ships to pass beneath, a choreography of engineering that turns functionality into art. The neo-Gothic towers that flank the bridge, adorned with intricate details, evoke the romantic spirit of an age that balanced progress with aesthetics.

As you picture yourself walking across the Tower Bridge's suspended walkways, imagine the architects who envisioned its innovative design, the workers who toiled to bring it to life. The Tower Bridge isn't just a bridge; it's a testament to the fusion of imagination and practicality that drives human progress.

Yet, its significance reaches beyond its functional purpose. The Tower Bridge isn't just a transportation link; it's a London landmark that echoes with the footsteps of generations. It's a reminder of London's historic heart, a living witness to the city's evolution and a testament to the enduring relevance of architectural vision.

Dreamers and advocates of progress, let the Tower Bridge's elegant mechanism inspire your creative journey. Just as its drawbridges rise and fall, so too can your creations adapt to the changing currents of time and need. The bridge's story whispers that every project you undertake, every innovation you pioneer, can be a step toward connecting the threads of the human narrative.

As you contemplate the Tower Bridge's majestic span against London's skyline, remember that it's more than just a bridge; it's a testament to the power of ingenuity and the spirit of connection. Let its legacy encourage you to design not just for the present, but for the tomorrows that await – for just as the Tower Bridge's bascules rise to welcome ships, so too can your creations rise to meet the challenges and opportunities that lie ahead, anchoring the spirit of progress and unity in the grand tapestry of existence.

26

Golden Gate Bridge, USA

Amid the mist-kissed embrace of San Francisco's bay and the grandeur of the Pacific coast, a bridge of pure elegance and engineering marvel rises as a gateway to dreams – the Golden Gate Bridge. This iconic structure isn't just a bridge; it's a symphony of innovation, a testament to human ingenuity that links not just land, but hearts and aspirations across time and space.

Imagine an era when the world was grappling with the Great Depression and the Golden Gate Bridge emerged as a beacon of hope and progress. Completed in the 1930s, this suspension bridge wasn't just a passage; it was a declaration of resilience. The Golden Gate Bridge isn't just a structure; it's a testament to the tenacity of human endeavor, to the audacious spirit that rises in the face of adversity.

The Golden Gate Bridge's design isn't just architecture; it's a dance of cables and towers, a feat of engineering poetry. Its vivid orange hue, chosen both for visibility in the fog and to complement the surrounding landscape, stands as a beacon of optimism against the backdrop of the bay. The sweeping curve of the bridge's main span, the graceful lines of its art deco towers, all come together to form a harmonious union of aesthetics and functionality.

As you picture yourself walking or driving across the Golden Gate Bridge's expanse, imagine the architects who dared to bridge the formidable gap, the workers who labored amidst the swirling tides. The Golden Gate Bridge isn't just a bridge; it's a tribute to the audacity of imagination and the sweat of determination.

Yet, its significance stretches far beyond its functional purpose. The Golden Gate Bridge isn't just a transportation link; it's an emblem of San Francisco's spirit, a symbol of unity and a testament to the enduring power of shared dreams. It has watched over decades of history, from wartime to technological leaps, reminding us that we can forge connections even when faced with seemingly insurmountable challenges.

Dreamers and creators of possibility, let the Golden Gate Bridge's majestic span inspire your own creative endeavors. Just as its towers rise to touch the sky, so too can your creations reach new heights, transcending limitations and stretching the boundaries of what's possible. The bridge's story whispers that every venture you undertake, every dream you nurture, can be a bridge that connects aspirations and propels them forward.

As you contemplate the Golden Gate Bridge's breathtaking sweep against the canvas of the bay, remember that it's more than just a bridge; it's a reminder that even in the midst of stormy waters, humanity's spirit can rise and build marvels that span generations. Let its legacy encourage you to design not just for function, but for the elevation of human aspirations – for just as the Golden Gate Bridge's cables weave a path across the bay, so too can your creations weave a tapestry of innovation and progress in the grand journey of existence.

27

Shard, UK

Amidst the urban tapestry of London's skyline, a shard of glass and steel pierces the heavens with audacity and grace – The Shard. This iconic skyscraper isn't just a building; it's a symphony of modernity, a testament to human ambition that reaches for the sky while grounding itself in the spirit of innovation.

Imagine a world where the city's pulse matched the rhythm of progress, and The Shard emerged as a beacon of contemporary architecture. Completed in the 21st century, this tower wasn't just a structure; it was a proclamation of urban sophistication. The Shard isn't just a building; it's a fusion of design and aspiration that embraces the city's heartbeat while reflecting the boundless possibilities of the future.

The Shard's design isn't just architecture; it's a marvel of glass and light, a fusion of aesthetics and functionality. Its pyramid-like form tapers skyward, as if echoing the aspirations that can rise above limitations. The glass façade captures London's ever-changing skies, blurring the boundaries between the tower and the elements.

As you picture yourself ascending The Shard's levels and gazing across London's panorama, imagine the architects who dared to challenge the sky, the engineers who turned the vision into reality. The Shard isn't just a skyscraper; it's a testament to the fusion of vision and skill, a monument to human ability to rise above the ordinary.

Yet, its significance resonates beyond its towering presence. The Shard isn't just a building; it's a symbol of London's modernity, a celebration of its spirit of innovation. It's a testament to the city's ability to blend history with the cutting edge, reminding us that progress doesn't mean severing ties with the past, but rather building upon the foundation of heritage.

Dreamers and visionaries, let The Shard's upward thrust inspire your creative pursuits. Just as its sleek design pierces the sky, so too can your creations transcend the limitations of convention. The tower's story whispers that every endeavor you undertake, every project you nurture, can be a testament to the audacious power of human imagination.

As you contemplate The Shard's gleaming form against the London backdrop, remember that it's more than just a skyscraper; it's a reminder that cities evolve, dreams evolve, and the potential to shape a better future is limitless. Let its legacy encourage you to design not just for the present, but for the innovations that will shape tomorrow – for just as The Shard reaches for the heavens, so too can your creations inspire generations and propel human progress in the grand symphony of existence.

28

CN Tower, Canada

Amid the vibrant embrace of Toronto's cityscape and the vast expanse of the Great White North, a tower of steel and imagination soars towards the sky – the CN Tower. This iconic structure isn't just a tower; it's a symphony of engineering and audacity, a testament to human ingenuity that reaches beyond the clouds while remaining firmly grounded in a city's heart.

CN TOWER, CANADA

Imagine a world where the skyline met the horizon with innovation, and the CN Tower emerged as a beacon of Canada's ambitions. Completed in the 1970s, this tower wasn't just an observation point; it was a declaration of Canada's prowess. The CN Tower isn't just a structure; it's a melding of technical excellence and national pride, a monument to a country's desire to touch the skies.

The CN Tower's design isn't just architecture; it's a fusion of functionality and aesthetics, a marvel of form following function. Its needle-like spire rises like an arrow, pointing both to the heavens and to the ideals of progress. The glass-floored observation decks offer an awe-inspiring view that connects visitors with both the city below and the infinite horizons beyond.

As you picture yourself ascending the CN Tower's elevators and looking out at Toronto's panorama, imagine the engineers who envisioned its towering form, the builders who raised it skyward. The CN Tower isn't just a tower; it's a testament to the collaborative effort of countless minds and hands, a testament to the spirit of teamwork and determination.

Yet, its significance stretches beyond its impressive height. The CN Tower isn't just an observation point; it's an emblem of Toronto's identity, a symbol of Canada's place on the global stage. It stands as a beacon that welcomes travelers and a vantage point that allows us to see the city from new perspectives.

Dreamers and innovators, let the CN Tower's lofty spire inspire your own creative pursuits. Just as its form reaches beyond the ordinary, so too can your creations transcend limitations. The tower's story whispers that every endeavor you embark upon, every idea you nurture, can be a tribute to the human drive to push boundaries.

As you contemplate the CN Tower's majestic silhouette against Toronto's skyline, remember that it's more than just a tower; it's a symbol of human potential and the desire to reach for new heights. Let its legacy inspire you to design not just for the present, but for the aspirations that will guide us towards the limitless possibilities of the future – for just as the CN Tower's spire touches the sky, so too can your creations touch the realms of imagination and innovation in the grand tapestry of existence.

29

Pyramids of Teotihuacan, Mexico

Amid the ancient windswept plains of Mexico, a city of mysteries and marvels rises from the earth with grandeur and enigma – the Pyramids of Teotihuacan. These iconic structures aren't just pyramids; they are the guardians of a lost civilization's secrets, a testament to human ambition that defies the passage of time and beckons us to ponder the heights of human achievement.

Imagine an era when the sun-kissed land cradled a civilization of visionaries, and Teotihuacan stood as a bustling metropolis. Flourishing from the 1st to the 7th century AD, this city wasn't just a settlement; it was a hub of culture and commerce. The Pyramids of Teotihuacan aren't just structures; they are echoes of a civilization's aspirations and its connection to the cosmos.

The Pyramids of Teotihuacan's design isn't just architecture; it's a symphony of geometry and symbolism, an ode to the heavens and the Earth. The Pyramid of the Sun, with its colossal dimensions, rises to greet the celestial bodies, while the Pyramid of the Moon stands as a guardian to the mysteries of the cosmos. The Avenue of the Dead, stretching between them, whispers of processions and rituals that have become part of the land's lore.

As you picture yourself ascending the stone steps of the pyramids, imagine the hands that carved the stones, the minds that conceived their layout. The Pyramids of Teotihuacan aren't just archaeological remnants; they are a testament to the human desire to understand the universe and leave a mark upon the sands of time.

Yet, their significance reaches far beyond the boundaries of their age. The Pyramids of Teotihuacan aren't just ancient structures; they are a UNESCO World Heritage Site and a testament to the power of human preservation. They inspire us to explore our own histories, to cherish the legacies left by those who came before us.

Dreamers and seekers of knowledge, let the Pyramids of Teotihuacan's ancient whispers guide your own quests. Just as their layout mirrors the cosmos, so too can your creations reflect the beauty of the natural world. The pyramids' story whispers that every question you ask, every pursuit you undertake, can be a step towards unraveling the tapestry of existence.

PYRAMIDS OF TEOTIHUACAN, MEXICO

As you contemplate the Pyramid of the Sun and the Pyramid of the Moon against the Mexican horizon, remember that they are more than just ancient structures; they are gateways to another time, urging us to ponder the marvels of human creation. Let their legacy inspire you to design not just for aesthetics, but for the exploration of human potential and the mysteries that await our discovery – for just as the Pyramids of Teotihuacan stand as sentinels of an ancient age, so too can your creations stand as guardians of imagination and enlightenment in the grand journey of existence.

30

Kremlin, Russia

Amidst the historic heart of Moscow, where stories of empires and revolutions intertwine, a fortress of grandeur and power stands as a sentinel of Russia's past and present – the Kremlin. This iconic complex isn't just a fortress; it's a living chronicle of a nation's evolution, a tapestry of history woven into stone and gold, a testament to the endurance of a people and their aspirations.

KREMLIN, RUSSIA

Imagine a realm where czars and leaders shaped destinies, and the Kremlin emerged as a nucleus of power. Founded in the 12th century, this fortress wasn't just a stronghold; it was a citadel of authority and culture. The Kremlin isn't just a complex; it's a repository of centuries, a canvas on which Russia's story is painted in vibrant strokes.

The Kremlin's design isn't just architecture; it's a convergence of architectural styles, a collage of history's layers. The majestic spires of its cathedrals, the grandeur of its palaces, the towering red walls that encircle it all, evoke a sense of timelessness and authority. The intricate details of its churches' golden domes whisper of devotion and artistic brilliance.

As you picture yourself walking through the Kremlin's majestic gates and wandering its courtyards, imagine the hands that shaped its walls, the rulers who left their mark on its stones. The Kremlin isn't just a fortress; it's a testament to the aspirations and complexities of nation-building, a witness to the rise and fall of dynasties.

Yet, its significance spans far beyond the confines of history. The Kremlin isn't just an ancient complex; it's a UNESCO World Heritage Site and a symbol of Russia's identity and strength. It has witnessed eras of conflict, moments of unity, and stands as a reminder that the pages of history hold both lessons and inspiration for the present and future.

Dreamers and stewards of legacy, let the Kremlin's grandeur inspire your own creative journey. Just as its walls have witnessed generations, so too can your creations carry the spirit of time and stories. The Kremlin's story whispers that every endeavor you undertake, every work of art you craft, can be a reflection of the values and dreams that shape humanity.

As you contemplate the Kremlin's towers against Moscow's skyline, remember that it's more than just a fortress; it's a testament to human resilience and the spirit of continuity. Let its legacy encourage you to design not just for the moment, but for the endurance of culture, wisdom, and aspirations – for just as the Kremlin's walls have stood strong through the ages, so too can your creations stand as monuments of inspiration and heritage in the grand mosaic of existence.

31

Sydney Harbour Bridge, Australia

Amid the sun-kissed embrace of Sydney's harbor, a marvel of steel and vision stretches its arches towards the sky – the Sydney Harbour Bridge. This iconic structure isn't just a bridge; it's a symphony of engineering and aspiration, a connection between the shores and a metaphor for the journey of a nation and its people.

Imagine a world where a young nation was taking its first steps into the modern era, and the Sydney Harbour Bridge emerged as a symbol of progress and unity. Completed in the 1930s, this bridge wasn't just a means of transportation; it was a triumph of human endeavor over nature's obstacles. The Sydney Harbour Bridge isn't just a structure; it's a testament to the tenacity of a nation and its will to forge ahead.

The Sydney Harbour Bridge's design isn't just architecture; it's a harmonious blend of aesthetics and innovation, an artful feat of functionality. Its towering arch rises like an embrace, linking Sydney's central business district with the North Shore. The bridge's steel girders and rivets create an intricate pattern that speaks of both the human touch and the soaring possibilities of progress.

As you picture yourself walking or driving across the Sydney Harbour Bridge's expanse, imagine the engineers who conceived its design, the workers who labored with sweat and determination. The Sydney Harbour Bridge isn't just a bridge; it's a tribute to the marriage of imagination and hard work, a monument to human collaboration and ambition.

Yet, its significance echoes beyond its physical structure. The Sydney Harbour Bridge isn't just a transportation link; it's an emblem of Sydney's spirit, a symbol of Australia's modern identity. It's a beacon that welcomes travelers and a canvas for national celebrations, embodying the nation's spirit of embracing the future while honoring its past.

Dreamers and pioneers, let the Sydney Harbour Bridge's graceful arch inspire your creative pursuits. Just as its curve spans the waters, so too can your creations bridge gaps and connect hearts. The bridge's story whispers that every endeavor you embark upon, every dream you nurture, can be a tribute to the power of persistence and the ability to overcome challenges.

As you contemplate the Sydney Harbour Bridge's elegant silhouette against the backdrop of the harbor, remember that it's more than just a bridge; it's a symbol of the human spirit's capacity to shape the world around us. Let its legacy encourage you to design not just for function, but for the harmony of progress and aesthetics – for just as the Sydney Harbour Bridge unites two shores, so too can your creations unite dreams and realities in the grand voyage of existence.

32

Mont Saint-Michel, France

Amid the misty embrace of France's northern coastline, a mystical abbey seems to rise from the very sea itself – Mont Saint-Michel. This iconic structure isn't just an abbey; it's a testament to the marriage of nature and human ingenuity, a spiritual beacon that defies the tides of time and beckons us to explore the heights of faith and artistry.

Imagine an era when faith was the compass guiding lives, and Mont Saint-Michel stood as a sanctuary of devotion and architectural brilliance. Established in the 8th century, this abbey wasn't just a place of worship; it was a fortress of the soul. Mont Saint-Michel isn't just a structure; it's a monument to the enduring human connection to the divine and the mastery of adapting to nature's embrace.

Mont Saint-Michel's design isn't just architecture; it's a symphony of spirituality and strategic thinking, a poetic blend of human creativity and the sublime beauty of the natural world. Perched atop a rocky outcrop, the abbey seems to defy gravity itself. Its winding streets and structures cling to the rock, creating a microcosm of medieval life within its walls.

As you picture yourself ascending Mont Saint-Michel's winding paths and entering its hallowed halls, imagine the monks who sought solace there, the builders who labored amidst the salt-sprayed winds. Mont Saint-Michel isn't just an abbey; it's a testament to the devotion of generations, a physical embodiment of spiritual aspiration and the power of human hands to shape a legacy.

Yet, its significance spans far beyond the walls of its abbey. Mont Saint-Michel isn't just a place of worship; it's a UNESCO World Heritage Site and a living illustration of humanity's ability to harmonize with nature's rhythms. It stands as a reminder that our greatest creations are often those that resonate with the environment, enriching both the human experience and the natural landscape.

Dreamers and seekers of beauty, let Mont Saint-Michel's rugged splendor inspire your own creative quests. Just as its abbey seems to grow from the rock, so too can your creations emerge organically from the fertile soil of your imagination. The abbey's story whispers that every endeavor you undertake, every masterpiece you craft, can be a reflection of the soul's longing for transcendence.

As you contemplate Mont Saint-Michel's silhouette against the backdrop of the sea, remember that it's more than just an abbey; it's a testament to the eternal dance between the spiritual and the earthly. Let its legacy encourage you to design not just for function, but for the elevation of the human spirit and the harmonious interplay between human creation and the natural world – for just as Mont Saint-Michel stands as a sentinel of faith and artistry, so too can your creations stand as guardians of inspiration and beauty in the grand tapestry of existence.

33

Great Wall of China, China

Amid the ancient landscapes of China, a colossal testament to human determination and unity stretches across mountains and valleys – the Great Wall of China. This iconic structure isn't just a wall; it's a living chronicle of history's tapestry, a monument to the enduring spirit of a civilization that dared to transcend borders and challenges.

Imagine a time when kingdoms and dynasties sought to protect their realm, and the Great Wall of China emerged as a barrier of strength and symbolism. Constructed over centuries, this wall wasn't just a defensive structure; it was a symbol of a nation's resolve. The Great Wall of China isn't just a monument; it's a fusion of architectural ingenuity and the relentless pursuit of security and unity.

The Great Wall's design isn't just architecture; it's a marriage of geography and strategy, a testament to the power of collaboration. Its serpentine form winds through mountains and deserts, following the natural contours of the land. Watchtowers and fortifications stand like guardians along its length, evoking a sense of both defense and communication.

As you picture yourself walking along the Great Wall's ancient stones, imagine the laborers who hauled bricks, the engineers who mapped its course. The Great Wall of China isn't just a wall; it's a tribute to the sweat and sacrifice of countless hands, a tribute to the human will to overcome obstacles for the sake of a shared dream.

Yet, its significance echoes far beyond its defensive purpose. The Great Wall of China isn't just a barricade; it's a UNESCO World Heritage Site and a symbol of China's enduring identity. It speaks of a nation's commitment to unity, a reminder that the threads of history weave a narrative that transcends time and borders.

Dreamers and builders, let the Great Wall's vast expanse inspire your creative ventures. Just as its fortifications spanned thousands of miles, so too can your creations bridge gaps and connect cultures. The wall's story whispers that every endeavor you embark upon, every project you nurture, can be a testament to the power of human collaboration and the quest for shared aspirations.

As you contemplate the Great Wall of China's monumental presence against the landscape, remember that it's more than just a wall; it's a tribute to the human spirit's ability to envision and create. Let its legacy encourage you to design not just for the present, but for the ideals that transcend time – for just as the Great Wall of China unites disparate parts of a nation, so too can your creations unite hearts and dreams in the grand journey of existence.

34

Grand Central Terminal, USA

Amidst the bustling heart of New York City, a cathedral of transportation stands as a testament to the energy and dreams of a metropolis – the Grand Central Terminal. This iconic structure isn't just a train station; it's a symphony of architecture and urban life, a testament to human ambition that echoes the city's heartbeat and reaches for the future.

Imagine a time when the world was in motion, and Grand Central Terminal emerged as a hub of connections and possibilities. Opened in the early 20th century, this terminal wasn't just a stop; it was a gateway to dreams and destinations. The Grand Central Terminal isn't just a transportation hub; it's a testament to the dynamism of a city and its unyielding spirit.

The Grand Central Terminal's design isn't just architecture; it's a dance of grandeur and detail, a fusion of aesthetics and functionality. Its celestial ceiling stretches overhead, a vault of constellations that remind us of the grand scope of existence. The opulent main concourse, with its chandeliers and marble, evokes the city's aspirations to elegance and innovation.

As you picture yourself walking through the Grand Central Terminal's majestic halls and catching glimpses of the celestial mural above, imagine the architects who sought to shape a space that mirrors the city's diversity and grandeur, the workers who dedicated their craft to its construction. The Grand Central Terminal isn't just a building; it's a tribute to the human drive to connect, to traverse boundaries and unite lives.

Yet, its significance resonates beyond its architectural brilliance. The Grand Central Terminal isn't just a transportation hub; it's a beloved New York landmark and a living crossroads of lives and stories. It's a testament to the city's resilience and a reminder that amidst the fast-paced world, there's beauty in the connections we make.

Dreamers and city dwellers, let the Grand Central Terminal's bustling energy inspire your own creative pursuits. Just as its arches and vaults cradle lives in motion, so too can your creations hold the dreams of countless souls. The terminal's story whispers that every endeavor you undertake, every creation you bring to life, can be a reflection of the human desire to reach out and make a mark in the world.

As you contemplate the Grand Central Terminal's elegant façade amidst the city's skyline, remember that it's more than just a train station; it's a beacon of urban life and a testament to human connections. Let its legacy encourage you to design not just for the moment, but for the enduring threads that bind us together – for just as the Grand Central Terminal welcomes travelers from all walks of life, so too can your creations embrace the diverse tapestry of human existence in the grand mosaic of history.

35

Petronas Towers, Malaysia

Amidst the vibrant cityscape of Kuala Lumpur, a pair of majestic towers rise towards the heavens in a harmonious embrace – the Petronas Towers. These iconic structures aren't just buildings; they are a symphony of modernity and cultural pride, a testament to human innovation that reaches for the sky while paying homage to Malaysia's heritage.

Imagine a realm where traditions dance with progress, and the Petronas Towers emerged as a beacon of Malaysia's aspirations. Completed in the 1990s, these towers weren't just skyscrapers; they were a declaration of Malaysia's global presence. The Petronas Towers aren't just buildings; they are a marriage of architectural brilliance and a nation's identity.

The Petronas Towers' design isn't just architecture; it's a fusion of geometric elegance and cultural symbolism, a tribute to the values that define Malaysia. Their sleek and futuristic forms are a testament to human engineering and vision, while the Islamic-inspired patterns that adorn them reflect the nation's heritage.

As you picture yourself standing at the base of the Petronas Towers and gazing upwards, imagine the architects who dared to dream of such heights, the engineers who transformed those dreams into reality. The Petronas Towers aren't just steel and glass; they are an ode to the human pursuit of the extraordinary, a tribute to the dedication of those who crafted their magnificence.

Yet, their significance resonates beyond their physical presence. The Petronas Towers aren't just landmarks; they are a symbol of Malaysia's emergence onto the global stage and a representation of the nation's unity amidst diversity. They remind us that modernity can coexist harmoniously with tradition, and that a nation's identity is not lost amidst progress.

Dreamers and creators, let the Petronas Towers' twin silhouettes inspire your own aspirations. Just as they stand united yet distinct, so too can your creations reflect the beauty of individuality within a collective vision. The towers' story whispers that every endeavor you embark upon, every project you breathe life into, can be a testament to the harmonious dance between innovation and heritage.

PETRONAS TOWERS, MALAYSIA

As you contemplate the Petronas Towers' gleaming façade against the city's backdrop, remember that they're more than just buildings; they're a representation of human imagination and a celebration of cultural roots. Let their legacy encourage you to design not just for function, but for the synthesis of tradition and progress – for just as the Petronas Towers reach towards the skies, so too can your creations rise to inspire generations and shape the narrative of existence.

36

The White House, USA

Amid the storied avenues of Washington, D.C., a symbol of democracy and leadership stands with elegance and authority – the White House. This iconic structure isn't just a residence; it's a living testament to a nation's ideals, a beacon of hope and governance that has witnessed the unfolding history of a great land.

Imagine a time when a young nation was forging its path, and the White

House emerged as a cornerstone of leadership and vision. Completed in the late 18th century, this building wasn't just a home; it was a symbol of America's journey towards liberty and unity. The White House isn't just a structure; it's a testament to the values that define a nation and its aspirations.

The White House's design isn't just architecture; it's a balance of grandeur and approachability, a canvas that showcases both leadership and openness. Its iconic neoclassical façade, with its columns and porticos, echoes the democracy of ancient Greece and Rome. The building's symmetry and proportions evoke a sense of stability and order.

As you picture yourself standing in front of the White House's portico and gazing at the North Lawn, imagine the architects who envisioned this emblem of leadership, the artisans who meticulously shaped its details. The White House isn't just a building; it's a testament to the visionaries and craftsmen who shaped a symbol that resonates with generations.

Yet, its significance expands far beyond its physical presence. The White House isn't just a presidential residence; it's a symbol of the nation's democracy, a focal point for citizens and leaders alike. It serves as a reminder that the course of history is charted by leaders and their commitment to the well-being of the nation.

Dreamers and advocates of change, let the White House's columns inspire your own journeys. Just as they stand as pillars of democratic ideals, so too can your creations be the pillars that uphold the values you hold dear. The White House's story whispers that every endeavor you undertake, every effort you invest, can be a tribute to the power of leadership and the pursuit of a better world.

As you contemplate the White House's iconic silhouette against the National Mall's expanse, remember that it's more than just a residence; it's a testament to the potential of individuals to shape a nation's destiny. Let its legacy encourage you to design not just for aesthetics, but for the enduring principles that guide us towards progress – for just as the White House stands as a sentinel of democracy, so too can your creations stand as beacons of inspiration and change in the grand tapestry of history.

37

Big Ben, UK

Amid the historic embrace of London's skyline, a tower stands as a timeless guardian of time and tradition – Big Ben. This iconic structure isn't just a clock tower; it's a symphony of history and innovation, a sentinel that chimes across generations and invites us to contemplate the fleeting beauty of existence.

Imagine an era when the world was abuzz with change, and Big Ben's resonant chimes emerged as a signature of London's identity. Erected in the 19th century, this tower wasn't just a timekeeper; it was a melody that echoed the pulse of a city. Big Ben isn't just a clock; it's a testament to human precision and a city's heartbeat.

Big Ben's design isn't just architecture; it's a fusion of Gothic grandeur and functional elegance, an epitome of Victorian engineering. Its towering form and intricate ornamentation evoke a sense of timelessness, while the clock's four faces diligently mark the passage of hours. The tower's belfry houses the resounding bell that has become synonymous with the name "Big Ben."

As you picture yourself strolling along the River Thames and gazing at Big Ben's majestic presence, imagine the architects who wove history into its stones, the clockmakers who brought precision to its mechanisms. Big Ben isn't just a tower; it's a monument to the collective effort of visionaries and craftsmen who shaped an icon that stands as a bridge between eras.

Yet, its significance extends beyond its iconic profile. Big Ben isn't just a timepiece; it's a symbol of London's endurance and resilience. It has weathered wars and witnessed celebrations, and its chimes have served as a backdrop to moments both personal and historic. It reminds us that amidst the march of time, certain landmarks anchor us to our roots.

Dreamers and admirers of beauty, let Big Ben's resounding chimes inspire your own creative pursuits. Just as its bell marks the cadence of time, so too can your creations echo the rhythm of your aspirations. Big Ben's story whispers that every endeavor you embark upon, every creation you breathe life into, can be a tribute to the exquisite symphony of existence.

As you contemplate Big Ben's majestic silhouette against the London sky, remember that it's more than just a clock tower; it's a guardian of memories and a testament to human craftsmanship. Let its legacy encourage you to design not just for the present, but for the enduring echoes that connect us to history and inspire us to shape the future – for just as Big Ben's chimes resonate through the ages, so too can your creations leave an indelible mark in the grand tapestry of life.

38

St. Peter's Basilica, Vatican City

In the heart of Vatican City, where faith and art intertwine, a colossal masterpiece of devotion and architecture reaches towards the heavens – St. Peter's Basilica. This iconic structure isn't just a church; it's a symphony of spirituality and human achievement, a sanctuary that invites us to contemplate both the divine and the heights of human imagination.

ST. PETER'S BASILICA, VATICAN CITY

Imagine a world where faith was a guiding light, and St. Peter's Basilica emerged as a testament to the grandeur of both the spiritual and the artistic. Conceived in the Renaissance period, this basilica wasn't just a place of worship; it was a celebration of divine beauty in human form. St. Peter's Basilica isn't just a building; it's a fusion of religious devotion and creative genius.

St. Peter's Basilica's design isn't just architecture; it's a harmony of grandeur and intimacy, a canvas where the celestial and earthly converge. Its dome, an iconic feature that crowns the basilica, seems to ascend to the heavens like a prayer translated into stone. The intricacies of its façade and the majesty of its interior inspire awe and reverence.

As you picture yourself standing before St. Peter's Basilica's awe-inspiring entrance and gazing at its colossal dome, imagine the artists who envisioned its grandeur, the architects who brought their vision to life. St. Peter's Basilica isn't just a church; it's a tribute to the confluence of faith and artistry, a testament to human hands shaping the divine into physical form.

Yet, its significance resonates far beyond its architectural magnificence. St. Peter's Basilica isn't just a place of worship; it's a symbol of the Catholic Church's spiritual center and a touchstone for believers around the world. It has hosted the papal coronations, inspired countless pilgrimages, and witnessed moments that have left indelible marks on history.

Dreamers and seekers of beauty, let St. Peter's Basilica's celestial dome inspire your own creative quests. Just as it ascends towards the heavens, so too can your creations transcend the ordinary and reach for the extraordinary. The basilica's story whispers that every endeavor you embark upon, every creation you nurture, can be a reflection of the profound connection between the divine and the human.

As you contemplate St. Peter's Basilica's majestic silhouette against the

Roman sky, remember that it's more than just a church; it's a testament to humanity's capacity to channel the sacred into tangible form. Let its legacy encourage you to design not just for aesthetics, but for the elevation of the spirit and the harmonious interplay between faith and creativity – for just as St. Peter's Basilica stands as a sanctuary of devotion and beauty, so too can your creations stand as beacons of inspiration and wonder in the grand tapestry of existence.

39

The Guggenheim Museum Bilbao, Spain

Nestled in the heart of Bilbao, a sculptural marvel emerges like a beacon of imagination and artistry – The Guggenheim Museum Bilbao. This iconic structure isn't just a museum; it's a symphony of innovation and creativity, a testament to the transformative power of architecture that dares to challenge conventions and reshape the cultural landscape.

Imagine a time when cities sought to redefine their identities, and The Guggenheim Museum Bilbao emerged as a catalyst for change. Opened in the late 20th century, this museum wasn't just a repository of art; it was a declaration that Bilbao was embracing a new era of cultural significance. The Guggenheim Museum Bilbao isn't just a building; it's a fusion of artistic expression and urban renewal.

The Guggenheim Museum Bilbao's design isn't just architecture; it's a dance of fluidity and audacity, a marriage of form and function that redefines how we perceive space. Its undulating curves and titanium-clad surfaces evoke a sense of movement frozen in time. The museum's interior is a symphony of open spaces and flowing lines, inviting visitors to navigate art in a new way.

As you picture yourself standing before The Guggenheim Museum Bilbao's striking exterior and entering its luminous atrium, imagine the architect who dared to sculpt this masterpiece, the engineers who embraced unconventional materials. The museum isn't just a cultural space; it's an embodiment of the audacity to push boundaries, to create a structure that doesn't just house art but becomes a work of art itself.

Yet, its significance reaches beyond its architectural ingenuity. The Guggenheim Museum Bilbao isn't just a gallery; it's a symbol of a city's rebirth and a testament to how architecture can ignite cultural and economic revitalization. It's a reminder that creative endeavors can reshape the destiny of cities and elevate the quality of life for their citizens.

Dreamers and innovators, let The Guggenheim Museum Bilbao's sweeping lines inspire your own ventures. Just as it reimagines traditional architectural norms, so too can your creations challenge existing paradigms. The museum's story whispers that every endeavor you embark upon, every project you bring to life, can be a testament to the power of creativity to reshape landscapes and foster evolution.

As you contemplate The Guggenheim Museum Bilbao's avant-garde silhouette against the city's backdrop, remember that it's more than just a museum; it's a manifesto of the transformative potential of design. Let its legacy encourage you to design not just for aesthetics, but for the potency to redefine the realms in which we live and create – for just as The Guggenheim Museum Bilbao has redefined Bilbao's cultural identity, so too can your creations shape the narrative of progress and possibility in the grand tapestry of history.

40

Taipei 101, Taiwan

TAIPEI 101, TAIWAN

Amidst the bustling skyline of Taipei, a modern marvel pierces the heavens with grace and purpose – Taipei 101. This iconic structure isn't just a skyscraper; it's a testament to human ambition and harmony with nature, a tower that invites us to reach for the sky while remaining rooted in our earthbound origins.

Imagine a time when Taiwan was aspiring to join the global stage, and Taipei 101 emerged as a symbol of the nation's determination. Completed in the 21st century, this skyscraper wasn't just a building; it was a declaration that Taipei was a city that could touch the skies. Taipei 101 isn't just an edifice; it's a fusion of modernity and cultural resonance.

Taipei 101's design isn't just architecture; it's a marriage of engineering and spirituality, a dance between technology and tradition. Its pagoda-inspired form pays homage to ancient Asian wisdom, with eight segments representing abundance and prosperity. The tower's bamboo-like structural elements echo nature's strength and adaptability.

As you picture yourself gazing up at Taipei 101's towering form and marveling at its interplay of light and glass, imagine the architects who dared to conceive this vertical wonder, the engineers who balanced form with function. Taipei 101 isn't just a skyscraper; it's a tribute to the fusion of human ingenuity and the timeless principles that guide us.

Yet, its significance extends beyond its architectural grandeur. Taipei 101 isn't just a tower; it's a symbol of Taiwan's rise as an economic and technological powerhouse. It reflects the nation's ability to bridge the past with the future, honoring traditions while embracing progress. It's a beacon that invites visitors to contemplate both humanity's aspiration to touch the skies and our roots in the soil of tradition.

Dreamers and pioneers, let Taipei 101's soaring heights inspire your own journeys. Just as its form reaches upwards while drawing inspiration from nature, so too can your creations be an embodiment of aspiration grounded in the essence of authenticity. Taipei 101's story whispers that every endeavor you undertake, every project you invest in, can be a tribute to the balance between progress and heritage.

As you contemplate Taipei 101's elegant silhouette against the Taipei skyline, remember that it's more than just a skyscraper; it's a reflection of a nation's identity and resilience. Let its legacy encourage you to design not just for the present, but for the harmonious interplay between innovation and tradition – for just as Taipei 101 bridges the gap between earth and sky, so too can your creations bridge the gap between aspirations and reality in the grand narrative of existence.

41

The Parthenon, USA

Amid the enchanting allure of Nashville, a tribute to artistic harmony and intellectual pursuit stands tall and majestic – The Parthenon. This iconic structure isn't just a building; it's a symbol of cultural resonance and the eternal quest for enlightenment, a monument that invites us to embrace the wisdom of the past while celebrating the creative spirit of the present.

Wait, you mentioned "The Parthenon, USA," which refers to a specific replica of the Parthenon in Nashville, Tennessee. This full-scale replica isn't just a mere imitation; it's a homage to the classical masterpiece that once graced ancient Athens.

Imagine a time when the ancient Athenians were constructing a temple to honor their goddess Athena, and that majestic creation served as a guiding light for the world. The Parthenon in Athens, built in the 5th century BC, wasn't just a temple; it was a monument to the ideals of beauty, knowledge, and democracy. The Parthenon isn't just a building; it's a fusion of art, architecture, and cultural identity.

Now, the Parthenon in Nashville isn't just a replication; it's a tribute to that legacy. Completed in the 20th century, this structure wasn't just an architectural feat; it was a statement that art knows no boundaries and that the spirit of Athens' glory can echo across oceans and time. The Parthenon in Nashville isn't just a building; it's a bridge that connects continents and eras.

The Parthenon's design isn't just architecture; it's a homage to the Golden Age of Greece and an affirmation that beauty is a timeless language. Its elegant colonnades and pediments evoke a sense of symmetry and proportion that speaks to the essence of aesthetic harmony. The replica's dedication to detail seeks to revive the spirit of a masterpiece lost to history.

As you picture yourself standing before The Parthenon's majestic façade in Nashville and marveling at its imposing columns, imagine the artisans who painstakingly crafted its sculptures and the architects who recreated the aura of an ancient wonder. The Parthenon isn't just a structure; it's a living testament to the human desire to revive the past and honor its legacy.

Yet, its significance reverberates beyond its architectural replication. The Parthenon in Nashville isn't just a museum; it's a testament to the timeless value of culture and the pursuit of knowledge. It symbolizes the idea that art and history can be shared across borders, and it serves as an emblem of Nashville's commitment to nurturing the creative spirit.

Dreamers and enthusiasts of culture, let The Parthenon's iconic façade inspire your own creative ventures. Just as its pillars stand as sentinels of history, so too can your creations stand as guardians of tradition and innovation. The Parthenon's story whispers that every endeavor you embark upon, every project you invest in, can be a tribute to the universality of art and the enduring pursuit of knowledge.

As you contemplate The Parthenon's majestic form against the Nashville skyline, remember that it's more than just a replica; it's a beacon that celebrates the interconnectedness of humanity's cultural legacy. Let its legacy encourage you to design not just for aesthetics, but for the preservation of heritage and the celebration of artistic ingenuity – for just as The Parthenon in Nashville revives the spirit of the past, so too can your creations contribute to the living tapestry of history and inspiration.

42

Marina Bay Sands, Singapore

Amid the modern marvel of Singapore's skyline, a trio of towers cradle an otherworldly oasis – Marina Bay Sands. This iconic structure isn't just a hotel; it's a symphony of luxury and ingenuity, a destination that beckons us to dream beyond boundaries and reimagine what is possible when human creativity takes flight.

Imagine a time when Singapore was envisioning a landmark that would define its identity, and Marina Bay Sands emerged as a testament to the nation's audacious vision. Completed in the 21st century, this integrated resort wasn't just a complex; it was a statement that Singapore was embracing a future where innovation knows no limits. Marina Bay Sands isn't just a building; it's an epitome of elegance and ambition.

Marina Bay Sands' design isn't just architecture; it's a ballet of fluidity and grandeur, a convergence of form and function that captivates the imagination. Its three towers rise like sentinels, supporting a rooftop SkyPark that seems to hover above the cityscape. The SkyPark's infinity pool, suspended in mid-air, reflects the boundless possibilities that emerge when human imagination and engineering dance in harmony.

As you picture yourself gazing at Marina Bay Sands' iconic SkyPark from across the harbor or wandering through its luxurious interiors, imagine the architects who dared to dream up this oasis, the engineers who orchestrated the feat of creating a rooftop sanctuary unlike any other. Marina Bay Sands isn't just a resort; it's a testament to the marriage of innovation and opulence that defines Singapore's spirit.

Yet, its significance extends far beyond its architectural prowess. Marina Bay Sands isn't just a hotel; it's a symbol of Singapore's transformation from a bustling port city to a global hub of innovation and commerce. It stands as a beacon that draws travelers and thinkers to its embrace, inviting them to experience luxury and design at the intersection of cultures.

Dreamers and adventurers, let Marina Bay Sands' suspended pool inspire your own creative pursuits. Just as it defies gravity while inviting contemplation, so too can your creations transcend boundaries and inspire others to think beyond the conventional. Marina Bay Sands' story whispers that every endeavor you embark upon, every project you nurture, can be a tribute to the boundless potential of human ingenuity.

As you contemplate Marina Bay Sands' spectacular form against Singapore's skyline, remember that it's more than just a hotel; it's a symbol of a nation's determination to rewrite its narrative and lead with innovation. Let its legacy encourage you to design not just for aesthetics, but for the fusion of luxury and visionary thinking – for just as Marina Bay Sands redefined Singapore's skyline, so too can your creations redefine the limits of possibility in the grand tapestry of history.

43

Guggenheim Museum, USA (New York)

Amid the vibrant pulse of New York City, a spiraling temple of art rises with boundless creativity – the Guggenheim Museum. This iconic structure isn't just a museum; it's a symphony of artistic expression and architectural innovation, a sanctuary that invites us to explore the depths of human imagination while challenging the conventions of traditional design.

Imagine a time when the art world was seeking a canvas that could embrace modernity, and the Guggenheim Museum emerged as a testament to the transformative power of architecture. Opened in the mid-20th century, this museum wasn't just a space to house art; it was a declaration that New York City was at the forefront of cultural evolution. The Guggenheim Museum isn't just a building; it's a fusion of art, architecture, and the spirit of exploration.

The Guggenheim Museum's design isn't just architecture; it's a dance of curves and lines, a marriage of form and function that defies convention. Its spiraling ramp unfurls like a gallery of dreams, allowing visitors to ascend through layers of artistic narrative. The museum's circular geometry embodies the idea of continuous discovery, challenging the linear expectations of traditional exhibition spaces.

As you picture yourself strolling along the Guggenheim Museum's iconic ramp and gazing at the interplay of light and shadows, imagine the architect who dared to reshape the concept of a museum, the visionaries who believed in the power of a non-traditional approach. The Guggenheim Museum isn't just a cultural space; it's a testament to the audacity to reimagine the canvas upon which art is displayed.

Yet, its significance resonates far beyond its architectural boldness. The Guggenheim Museum isn't just a gallery; it's a symbol of New York's enduring dedication to artistic innovation and a beacon that draws creators and enthusiasts from across the globe. It's a reminder that art isn't just contained within frames; it can exist in the very space we traverse, transforming the act of viewing into an immersive experience.

Dreamers and lovers of art, let the Guggenheim Museum's spiraling form inspire your own creative journeys. Just as it defies straight lines in favor of a continuous flow, so too can your creations embrace unconventional paths and transcend the expected. The Guggenheim Museum's story whispers that every endeavor you embark upon, every project you pour your passion into, can be a tribute to the limitless possibilities of creative expression.

As you contemplate the Guggenheim Museum's iconic silhouette against New York's skyline, remember that it's more than just a cultural institution; it's a testament to the city's commitment to pushing the boundaries of artistic presentation. Let its legacy encourage you to design not just for aesthetics, but for the exploration of new horizons – for just as the Guggenheim Museum redefined the museum experience, so too can your creations redefine the way we perceive and interact with the world around us in the grand tapestry of history.

44

The Atomium, Belgium

Amidst the enchanting cityscape of Brussels, a magnificent structure emerges, transporting us into the realm of science and wonder – The Atomium. This iconic edifice isn't just a building; it's a symphony of scientific imagination and architectural audacity, a monument that beckons us to explore the mysteries of the universe while celebrating the boundless potential of human ingenuity.

Imagine a time when the world was captivated by the promise of scientific progress, and The Atomium emerged as a symbol of that excitement. Unveiled during the mid-20th century, this structure wasn't just a monument; it was a declaration that humanity was unlocking the secrets of the atom and entering an era of discovery. The Atomium isn't just an edifice; it's a fusion of art, science, and the spirit of exploration.

The Atomium's design isn't just architecture; it's a harmony of spheres and tubes, an embodiment of scientific concepts translated into tangible form. Its interconnected orbs replicate the structure of an iron crystal magnified 165 billion times, transforming the microscopic into the monumental. The structure's interplay of steel and glass embodies the notion of progress entwined with transparency.

As you picture yourself standing beneath The Atomium's colossal spheres and gazing up at its interlocking tubes, imagine the architects who dared to manifest this marvel, the visionaries who understood that architecture could be a tribute to scientific vision. The Atomium isn't just a monument; it's a celebration of the marriage between art and science, a testament to the power of human imagination.

Yet, its significance resonates far beyond its architectural ingenuity. The Atomium isn't just a sculpture; it's a symbol of Belgium's spirit of innovation and its embrace of scientific exploration. It stands as a beacon of unity, having been constructed for the 1958 World's Fair, signifying the global community's shared curiosity and quest for progress.

Dreamers and admirers of the unknown, let The Atomium's interconnected orbs inspire your own pursuits. Just as it magnifies the atomic structure into tangible wonder, so too can your creations shed light on the mysteries that captivate your mind. The Atomium's story whispers that every endeavor you embark upon, every project you invest in, can be a tribute to the convergence of knowledge and creative expression.

As you contemplate The Atomium's striking form against Brussels' skyline, remember that it's more than just a scientific tribute; it's a testament to humanity's relentless pursuit of understanding. Let its legacy encourage you to design not just for aesthetics, but for the celebration of curiosity and the exploration of the unknown – for just as The Atomium unveils the beauty of the microscopic world, so too can your creations unveil the beauty and wonder that lie within the grand tapestry of history.

45

Lotus Temple, India

Amidst the vibrant tapestry of New Delhi, a blossoming lotus emerges, inviting us to experience serenity and unity – the Lotus Temple. This iconic structure isn't just a temple; it's a sanctuary of peace and harmony, a haven that beckons us to connect with our inner selves while celebrating the beauty of diversity and the oneness of humanity.

Imagine a time when the world was seeking a sanctuary that transcended religious boundaries, and the Lotus Temple emerged as a symbol of universal spirituality. Completed in the 20th century, this architectural marvel wasn't just a place of worship; it was a testament that India was nurturing a space where people of all faiths could find solace and connection. The Lotus Temple isn't just a building; it's a fusion of spiritual resonance and architectural elegance.

The Lotus Temple's design isn't just architecture; it's a symphony of curves and petals, an embodiment of the lotus flower that holds deep spiritual significance in various cultures. Its pristine white form is a canvas that absorbs and reflects the changing hues of the sky, inviting contemplation and connection with the cosmos. The temple's circular geometry represents the interconnectedness of all paths to the divine.

As you picture yourself approaching the Lotus Temple's serene exterior and stepping into its tranquil interior, imagine the architects who envisioned this space of inclusivity, the visionaries who believed in the transformative power of architecture to unite hearts and minds. The Lotus Temple isn't just a place of worship; it's a tribute to the power of architecture to inspire a sense of unity and transcendence.

Yet, its significance reaches far beyond its architectural beauty. The Lotus Temple isn't just a religious space; it's a symbol of India's commitment to fostering harmony and understanding among people of different faiths. It stands as a reminder that places of worship can be gateways to a shared humanity, transcending the divisions that often separate us.

Dreamers and seekers of meaning, let the Lotus Temple's blossoming form inspire your own journeys. Just as it rises from the waters while representing purity, so too can your creations rise above challenges while embodying the essence of unity. The Lotus Temple's story whispers that every endeavor you embark upon, every project you invest in, can be a tribute to the potential of architecture to bring people together and inspire a sense of peace.

As you contemplate the Lotus Temple's graceful silhouette against New Delhi's skyline, remember that it's more than just a place of worship; it's a symbol of India's dedication to fostering harmony and embracing diversity. Let its legacy encourage you to design not just for aesthetics, but for the celebration of shared humanity and the cultivation of inner serenity – for just as the Lotus Temple welcomes all to its fold, so too can your creations embrace and uplift in the grand tapestry of history.

46

Casa Milà, Spain

In the heart of Barcelona's artistic soul, a living masterpiece of creativity and ingenuity graces the cityscape – Casa Milà, lovingly known as La Pedrera. This iconic structure isn't just a building; it's a symphony of artistic expression and architectural innovation, a canvas that invites us to explore the boundaries of design while celebrating the boundless power of human imagination.

Imagine a time when Barcelona was yearning for a structure that would redefine the concept of urban living, and Casa Milà emerged as a testament to the marriage of art and functionality. Constructed in the early 20th century, this architectural gem wasn't just an apartment building; it was a declaration that design could transcend the mundane and elevate daily life to an art form. Casa Milà isn't just an edifice; it's a fusion of aesthetics, functionality, and the spirit of artistic exploration.

Casa Milà's design isn't just architecture; it's a symphony of flowing lines and organic forms, an embodiment of the Art Nouveau movement that sought to integrate art into every aspect of life. Its undulating façade seems to ripple like a stone worn smooth by the sea, while its iron balconies and sculpted chimneys evoke a sense of living sculpture. The rooftop's surreal landscape, adorned with unconventional forms, stands as a testament to Gaudí's philosophy that architecture should imitate nature.

As you picture yourself strolling along Casa Milà's organic corridors and gazing at the rooftop's whimsical chimneys, imagine the architect who dared to redefine the possibilities of design, the artisans who crafted each intricate detail with unwavering dedication. Casa Milà isn't just a residence; it's a testament to the audacity to reimagine the spaces we inhabit and infuse them with beauty and creativity.

Yet, its significance resonates far beyond its architectural marvels. Casa Milà isn't just a building; it's a symbol of Barcelona's artistic heritage and its commitment to pushing the boundaries of conventional design. It stands as a reminder that architecture isn't just about erecting structures; it's about shaping experiences, emotions, and the very essence of urban existence.

Dreamers and admirers of the creative spirit, let Casa Milà's flowing forms inspire your own artistic journeys. Just as it marries art and function with seamless grace, so too can your creations embody the idea that functionality can be a canvas for artistic expression. Casa Milà's story whispers that every endeavor you embark upon, every project you invest in, can be a tribute to the fusion of aesthetics and functionality.

As you contemplate Casa Milà's sinuous contours against Barcelona's backdrop, remember that it's more than just a building; it's a living homage to artistic freedom and architectural innovation. Let its legacy encourage you to design not just for practicality, but for the celebration of artistic exploration and the reshaping of the spaces we inhabit – for just as Casa Milà reshaped Barcelona's skyline, so too can your creations reshape the world's perception of what's possible in the grand tapestry of history.

47

Empire State Building, USA

Amid the bustling rhythm of New York City, a towering beacon of aspiration and possibility graces the skyline – the Empire State Building. This iconic structure isn't just a skyscraper; it's a symphony of ambition and innovation, a testament that dares us to reach for the stars while honoring the grit and determination that define the American spirit.

Imagine a time when the world was emerging from the depths of the Great Depression, and the Empire State Building rose like a phoenix from adversity. Completed in the 20th century, this architectural marvel wasn't just a building; it was a declaration that even in the face of challenges, humanity could achieve the extraordinary. The Empire State Building isn't just an edifice; it's a fusion of architectural prowess, human tenacity, and the spirit of progress.

The Empire State Building's design isn't just architecture; it's a symphony of Art Deco elegance and engineering brilliance. Its towering form, adorned with cascading setbacks that soar into the heavens, reflects the audacity to build towards the sky. The building's spire, originally intended as a mooring mast for airships, symbolizes the spirit of exploration and the convergence of innovation with the practical.

As you picture yourself standing before the Empire State Building's grand entrance and gazing up at its iconic silhouette, imagine the architects who translated dreams into steel and stone, the workers who forged this icon under demanding conditions. The Empire State Building isn't just a structure; it's a tribute to the power of collective effort, resilience, and the pursuit of greatness.

Yet, its significance extends beyond its architectural magnificence. The Empire State Building isn't just a skyscraper; it's a symbol of New York City's resilience and its enduring role as a global epicenter of commerce, culture, and aspiration. It stands as a testament to the city's ability to adapt, evolve, and shape the trajectory of history.

Dreamers and seekers of achievement, let the Empire State Building's towering heights inspire your own pursuits. Just as it soars above the cityscape, so too can your aspirations rise above challenges and define new horizons. The Empire State Building's story whispers that every endeavor you embark upon, every project you invest in, can be a tribute to the indomitable human spirit and the pursuit of excellence.

As you contemplate the Empire State Building's majestic form against New York's bustling streets, remember that it's more than just a skyscraper; it's a living monument to human endeavor and the city's unyielding drive. Let its legacy encourage you to design not just for practicality, but for the elevation of human potential and the pursuit of greatness – for just as the Empire State Building touched the skies, so too can your creations touch the hearts and minds of generations in the grand tapestry of history.

48

Willis Tower (formerly Sears Tower), USA

Amidst the urban heartbeat of Chicago, a towering colossus of ambition and engineering prowess graces the skyline – the Willis Tower, known to many as the Sears Tower. This iconic structure isn't just a skyscraper; it's a symphony of human achievement and architectural innovation, a testament that urges us to reach for the sky while honoring the tireless spirit of progress.

Imagine a time when the world was captivated by the promise of architectural marvels, and the Willis Tower soared to life as a beacon of possibility. Completed in the 20th century, this architectural wonder wasn't just a building; it was a declaration that America's ambitions could touch the clouds. The Willis Tower isn't just an edifice; it's a fusion of vision, engineering excellence, and the spirit of human achievement.

The Willis Tower's design isn't just architecture; it's a symphony of steel and glass that defies gravity. Its towering form, stretching upwards with a confidence that embraces the sky, is a tribute to the audacity of human ambition. The iconic skydeck, suspended a quarter-mile above the ground, offers a breathtaking perspective that encapsulates the idea that challenges can be conquered, heights can be reached.

As you picture yourself standing at the foot of the Willis Tower and gazing up at its monumental presence, imagine the architects who dared to push the limits of what was possible, the workers who labored to transform dreams into reality. The Willis Tower isn't just a skyscraper; it's a homage to the synergy of human ingenuity, perseverance, and the pursuit of the extraordinary.

Yet, its significance stretches far beyond its towering heights. The Willis Tower isn't just a building; it's a symbol of Chicago's tenacity and its relentless drive to define modern skylines. It stands as a reminder that architecture isn't just about erecting structures; it's about building the future, cementing legacies, and leaving an indelible mark on history.

Dreamers and believers in the extraordinary, let the Willis Tower's soaring heights inspire your own pursuits. Just as it stands tall amidst the city's landscape, so too can your aspirations rise above challenges and define new paradigms. The Willis Tower's story whispers that every endeavor you embark upon, every project you invest in, can be a tribute to the courage to dream big and the conviction to make those dreams a reality.

As you contemplate the Willis Tower's monumental form against Chicago's bustling streets, remember that it's more than just a skyscraper; it's a symbol of humanity's unending quest for excellence and progress. Let its legacy encourage you to design not just for practicality, but for the elevation of human achievement and the relentless pursuit of the extraordinary – for just as the Willis Tower touches the heavens, so too can your creations touch the hearts and aspirations of generations in the grand tapestry of history.

49

Buckingham Palace, UK

In the heart of London, a regal masterpiece of history and tradition graces the landscape – Buckingham Palace. This iconic structure isn't just a palace; it's a living symbol of monarchy and national heritage, a majestic home that beckons us to journey through time while celebrating the enduring power of royalty.

Imagine a time when grandeur and elegance were intertwined with royal lives, and Buckingham Palace emerged as the sovereign's sanctuary. Standing as the official residence of the British monarch since the 19th century, this architectural jewel wasn't just a palace; it was a testament to the monarchy's role as the guardian of tradition and the heartbeat of a nation. Buckingham Palace isn't just an edifice; it's a fusion of history, pageantry, and the spirit of royal continuity.

Buckingham Palace's design isn't just architecture; it's a symphony of neoclassical elegance and royal splendor. Its grand façade, punctuated by stately columns and regal statuary, is a visual ode to the monarchy's significance. The palace's ceremonial balcony, where the royals appear during historic occasions, embodies a unique connection between the sovereign and their people.

As you picture yourself gazing at the majestic Buckingham Palace and imagining the elaborate ceremonies that unfold within its walls, think of the architects who crafted this palace as a canvas for history, the artisans who filled its interiors with exquisite details. Buckingham Palace isn't just a royal residence; it's a testament to the craftsmanship, dedication, and traditions that have been passed down through generations.

Yet, its significance extends beyond its regal façade. Buckingham Palace isn't just a building; it's a symbol of the British monarchy's role in shaping the country's identity and serving as a unifying force. It stands as a reminder that palaces aren't merely opulent residences; they are living museums of culture, time capsules of history that tell the story of a nation.

Dreamers and admirers of heritage, let Buckingham Palace's timeless elegance inspire your own journeys. Just as it stands as a testament to centuries of tradition, so too can your creations honor the legacies that shape your path. Buckingham Palace's story whispers that every endeavor you embark upon, every project you invest in, can be a tribute to the values, culture, and history that have guided you.

As you contemplate Buckingham Palace's stately presence against London's bustling backdrop, remember that it's more than just a royal residence; it's a symbol of continuity, unity, and the threads that bind a nation together. Let its legacy encourage you to design not just for aesthetics, but for the preservation of heritage and the celebration of cultural identity – for just as Buckingham Palace embodies the essence of monarchy, so too can your creations embody the essence of your own journey in the grand tapestry of history.

50

Milan Cathedral, Italy

In the heart of Milan, a soaring testament to faith and architectural magnificence graces the cityscape – the Milan Cathedral, affectionately known as the Duomo. This iconic structure isn't just a cathedral; it's a symphony of devotion and artistic brilliance, a spiritual sanctuary that invites us to contemplate the divine while marveling at the grandeur of human creativity.

Imagine a time when faith was a guiding force in the hearts of people, and the Milan Cathedral was conceived as a divine offering. Rising triumphantly since the 14th century, this architectural wonder wasn't just a place of worship; it was a declaration of the city's dedication to religious reverence and its commitment to crafting a spiritual masterpiece. The Milan Cathedral isn't just an edifice; it's a fusion of faith, architectural prowess, and the spirit of artistic devotion.

The Milan Cathedral's design isn't just architecture; it's a symphony of Gothic grandeur and intricate detailing. Its façade, adorned with an array of statues, reliefs, and spires that seem to reach for the heavens, is a testament to the devotion and meticulous craftsmanship that have gone into its creation. The cathedral's elaborate interior, featuring stunning stained glass windows and ornate altars, is a space that whispers of eternity and inspires reverence.

As you picture yourself standing before the Milan Cathedral's magnificent entrance and gazing up at its towering spires, imagine the architects who embarked on the monumental task of creating this sacred space, the artisans who poured their talents into every stone and carving. The Milan Cathedral isn't just a cathedral; it's a tribute to the power of human dedication, the quest for the divine, and the legacy of generations who worked to bring a spiritual vision to life.

Yet, its significance reaches far beyond its architectural splendor. The Milan Cathedral isn't just a religious site; it's a symbol of Milan's identity, its history, and its place as a cultural and spiritual epicenter. It stands as a reminder that cathedrals aren't just places of worship; they are repositories of culture, art, and the stories that have shaped communities for centuries.

Dreamers and seekers of meaning, let the Milan Cathedral's soaring spires inspire your own quests for understanding. Just as it reaches skyward in reverence, so too can your aspirations rise above challenges to touch the infinite. The Milan Cathedral's story whispers that every endeavor you embark upon, every project you invest in, can be a tribute to the connection between the human and the divine, and the transformative power of artistic dedication.

As you contemplate the Milan Cathedral's majestic form against Milan's bustling streets, remember that it's more than just a cathedral; it's a testament to the enduring legacy of faith, art, and community. Let its legacy encourage you to design not just for aesthetics, but for the elevation of the soul and the celebration of the profound connections that weave through the fabric of existence – for just as the Milan Cathedral reaches towards heaven, so too can your creations touch the hearts and spirits of generations in the grand tapestry of history.

51

Palace of Westminster, UK

In the heart of London, a majestic fortress of democracy and history rises above the River Thames – the Palace of Westminster. This iconic structure isn't just a parliament building; it's a living embodiment of the democratic spirit and architectural brilliance, a place that invites us to witness the power of collective decision-making while marveling at the fusion of artistic imagination and civic purpose.

Imagine a time when the pursuit of fair governance was taking root, and the Palace of Westminster was envisioned as a bastion of representation and discussion. Erected in the 19th century, this architectural gem wasn't just a government building; it was a testament that the voice of the people deserved a stately home, a place where laws were shaped and destinies decided. The Palace of Westminster isn't just an edifice; it's a harmonious blend of democracy, architectural elegance, and the spirit of shared governance.

The Palace of Westminster's design isn't just architecture; it's a symphony of neo-Gothic splendor and functional ingenuity. Its ornate façade, adorned with intricate stonework and pointed arches, resonates with echoes of medieval cathedrals. The iconic clock tower, housing the Big Ben bell, stands as a symbol of time's passage and the importance of timely decision-making in the corridors of power.

As you picture yourself standing before the Palace of Westminster's grand entrance and envisioning the debates and discussions that unfold within its walls, think of the architects who designed a palace that echoed the grandeur of history while serving the needs of a modern democracy. The Palace of Westminster isn't just a parliament building; it's a tribute to the delicate balance between tradition and progress, between history and the future.

Yet, its significance stretches far beyond its political function. The Palace of Westminster isn't just a building; it's a symbol of Britain's democratic values and its commitment to the rule of law. It stands as a reminder that parliament buildings aren't just halls of governance; they are living embodiments of the ideals that shape societies, nations, and the very essence of civil discourse.

Dreamers and advocates of change, let the Palace of Westminster's halls of debate inspire your own quests for impact. Just as it echoes with the voices of leaders and representatives, so too can your actions resonate in the grand arenas of change. The Palace of Westminster's story whispers that every endeavor you embark upon, every project you invest in, can be a tribute to the power of collaboration, the pursuit of fairness, and the drive to shape a better future.

As you contemplate the Palace of Westminster's majestic form against London's bustling streets, remember that it's more than just a government building; it's a testament to the principles of democracy, governance, and the delicate dance between authority and the people's will. Let its legacy encourage you to design not just for functionality, but for the elevation of civic engagement and the celebration of the voices that shape the course of history – for just as the Palace of Westminster echoes with debates, so too can your creations echo with the possibilities of progress in the grand tapestry of history.

52

Versailles Palace, France

In the enchanting landscapes of France, a symphony of elegance and opulence emerges – the Palace of Versailles. This iconic structure isn't just a palace; it's a living testament to the splendor of monarchy and the artistic heights that human creativity can ascend, a place that beckons us to step into the world of kings and queens while marveling at the grandeur of human imagination.

Imagine a time when monarchs sought to create expressions of their power and legacy, and the Palace of Versailles emerged as a grand vision brought to life. Rising to prominence in the 17th century, this architectural masterpiece wasn't just a residence; it was a declaration of royal authority and a canvas for the world's most exceptional artists to collaborate on a spectacle of unrivaled beauty. The Palace of Versailles isn't just an edifice; it's a harmonious blend of aristocratic grandeur, artistic genius, and the spirit of extravagance.

The Palace of Versailles' design isn't just architecture; it's a symphony of baroque and rococo styles that reflect the magnificence of the court. Its sprawling façade, adorned with ornate details, gilded accents, and expansive gardens, is an embodiment of the grandiose taste that defined an era. The Hall of Mirrors, with its mesmerizing mirrors and breathtaking frescoes, is a masterpiece that reflects the desire of the monarchy to showcase its wealth and power.

As you picture yourself wandering through the lavish halls and imagining the royal court in its resplendent glory, think of the architects who translated regal visions into stone and gardens, the artists who painted ceilings and sculpted fountains. The Palace of Versailles isn't just a palace; it's a tribute to the collaborations that birthed art, culture, and history that continues to enchant.

Yet, its significance stretches beyond its architectural grandeur. The Palace of Versailles isn't just a historic residence; it's a symbol of France's artistic and cultural legacy and its profound influence on the world's taste. It stands as a reminder that palaces aren't just structures of luxury; they are reflections of societies, narratives of power and beauty that shape human understanding.

Dreamers and admirers of beauty, let the Palace of Versailles' opulent interiors and sprawling gardens inspire your own quests for creative expression. Just as it transports you to the world of kings and queens, so too can your creations transport others to realms of imagination and wonder. The Palace of Versailles' story whispers that every endeavor you embark upon, every project you invest in, can be a tribute to the harmonious marriage of aesthetics and the celebration of human achievement.

As you contemplate the Palace of Versailles' lavish form against the backdrop of its expansive gardens, remember that it's more than just a palace; it's a legacy of elegance, artistic collaboration, and the magic of history. Let its legacy encourage you to design not just for functionality, but for the elevation of beauty, creativity, and the transformative power of shared vision – for just as the Palace of Versailles exudes majesty, so too can your creations exude the majesty of the human spirit in the grand tapestry of history.

53

Rila Monastery, Bulgaria

Nestled amidst the serene landscapes of Bulgaria, a haven of spirituality and architectural grace emerges – the Rila Monastery. This iconic structure isn't just a monastery; it's a testament to the enduring power of faith and the exquisite beauty that human hands can create, a place that invites us to pause in contemplation while marveling at the harmony between the divine and the earthly.

Imagine a time when monks sought solace in the embrace of nature, and the Rila Monastery was born as a sanctuary of prayer and devotion. Emerging in the 10th century, this architectural gem wasn't just a place of worship; it was a testament to the monk's quest for communion with the divine and their desire to craft a spiritual sanctuary that resonated with nature's serenity. The Rila Monastery isn't just an edifice; it's a harmonious blend of faith, cultural heritage, and the spirit of devotion.

The Rila Monastery's design isn't just architecture; it's a symphony of Byzantine and Bulgarian Renaissance styles that echo the beauty of faith. Its ornate façade, adorned with intricate frescoes and woodcarvings, reflects the meticulous craftsmanship that went into its creation. The central church, with its golden domes and ornamental elements, stands as a beacon of faith that reaches towards the heavens.

As you picture yourself standing before the Rila Monastery's majestic entrance and feel the aura of tranquility, envision the monks who found solace and enlightenment within its walls, the artisans who dedicated their lives to creating an oasis of spiritual beauty. The Rila Monastery isn't just a religious structure; it's a tribute to the symbiotic relationship between humanity and the divine, between the earthly and the ethereal.

Yet, its significance extends far beyond its spiritual purpose. The Rila Monastery isn't just a place of worship; it's a symbol of Bulgaria's cultural heritage and its enduring commitment to preserving its spiritual identity. It stands as a reminder that monasteries aren't just religious sites; they are repositories of traditions, guardians of history, and living embodiments of the values that shape societies.

Dreamers and seekers of inner peace, let the Rila Monastery's tranquil courtyards and adorned walls inspire your own quests for spiritual connection. Just as it emanates an aura of serenity, so too can your actions cultivate inner harmony and mindfulness. The Rila Monastery's story whispers that every endeavor you embark upon, every project you invest in, can be a tribute to the pursuit of inner enlightenment and the celebration of the connections between the human and the divine.

As you contemplate the Rila Monastery's timeless form against Bulgaria's natural beauty, remember that it's more than just a religious site; it's a testament to the union of faith, art, and nature. Let its legacy encourage you to design not just for aesthetics, but for the elevation of the soul and the celebration of the profound connections that weave through the fabric of existence – for just as the Rila Monastery touches the heart, so too can your creations touch the hearts and spirits of generations in the grand tapestry of history.

54

Burj al-Arab, UAE

Rising like a majestic sail above the sparkling waters of Dubai, the Burj al-Arab stands as a symbol of modern luxury and architectural audacity. This iconic structure isn't just a hotel; it's a testament to the boundless imagination of human achievement, a beacon of opulence that invites us to dream beyond horizons and marvel at the fusion of innovation and extravagance.

Imagine a time when the UAE sought to redefine the skyline with a daring vision, and the Burj al-Arab emerged as an icon of Dubai's global ambitions. Ascending to prominence in the late 20th century, this architectural marvel wasn't just a hotel; it was a declaration of Dubai's ascent as a hub of modernity, a place where hospitality and grandeur were elevated to new heights. The Burj al-Arab isn't just an edifice; it's a harmonious blend of contemporary flair, lavish design, and the spirit of limitless ambition.

The Burj al-Arab's design isn't just architecture; it's a symphony of audacious luxury and sleek lines that redefine the skyline. Its sail-shaped silhouette, adorned with an opulent helipad and shimmering glass façade, reflects the audacity of design and engineering that defied convention. The lavish interiors, featuring gold leaf accents and sumptuous materials, is a space that echoes indulgence and extravagance.

As you picture yourself standing before the Burj al-Arab's grand entrance and envisioning the world of luxury within, think of the architects who dared to transform Dubai's dreams into reality, the designers who meticulously curated opulent details. The Burj al-Arab isn't just a hotel; it's a tribute to the fusion of vision and execution, the power of imagination to transcend limits.

Yet, its significance stretches far beyond its luxurious offerings. The Burj al-Arab isn't just a hotel; it's a symbol of Dubai's meteoric rise as a global destination and its commitment to redefining the boundaries of possibility. It stands as a reminder that buildings aren't just structures; they are statements of progress, reflections of a city's aspirations, and ambassadors of innovation.

Dreamers and admirers of bold vision, let the Burj al-Arab's soaring height and unmatched extravagance inspire your own quests for pushing boundaries. Just as it reaches towards the heavens, so too can your aspirations reach beyond the ordinary. The Burj al-Arab's story whispers that every endeavor you embark upon, every project you invest in, can be a tribute to the audacious spirit, the courage to dream beyond convention, and the celebration of the extraordinary.

As you contemplate the Burj al-Arab's modern elegance against Dubai's dynamic backdrop, remember that it's more than just a hotel; it's a beacon of innovation, a symbol of aspiration, and a testament to the belief that dreams can be realized against all odds. Let its legacy encourage you to design not just for functionality, but for the elevation of imagination, ambition, and the transformative power of boldness in the grand tapestry of history.

55

Metropol Parasol, Spain

Imagine wandering through the heart of Seville, Spain, and stumbling upon a truly mesmerizing spectacle – the Metropol Parasol. This iconic structure isn't just an architectural wonder; it's a beacon of modernity and innovation that invites us to rethink the boundaries of design and reimagine the possibilities of urban spaces, all while marveling at the marriage of creativity and engineering.

Picture a time when a city square was transformed into a realm of artistic expression and functional space, and the Metropol Parasol came to life as a testament to contemporary architecture. Emerging in the 21st century, this architectural marvel wasn't just a structure; it was a declaration of Seville's willingness to embrace the new and the bold, a place where tradition and modernity converged in a remarkable way. The Metropol Parasol isn't just an edifice; it's a fusion of architectural innovation, urban rejuvenation, and the spirit of reimagining possibilities.

The Metropol Parasol's design isn't just architecture; it's a symphony of organic forms and daring curves that seem to defy gravity. Its intricate latticework, resembling a massive wooden mushroom, is a visual feast that engages the senses and reinterprets public spaces. The sweeping viewpoints atop the structure offer panoramic vistas of Seville's historic beauty, encouraging contemplation and a fresh perspective on the urban landscape.

As you picture yourself strolling beneath the Metropol Parasol's soaring canopy and feel the sunlight filtering through the lattice, think of the architect's bold vision, the engineers who turned concepts into reality. The Metropol Parasol isn't just a piece of art; it's a tribute to the power of collaboration, the ability of design to reshape urban experiences.

Yet, its significance transcends its innovative form. The Metropol Parasol isn't just an architectural curiosity; it's a symbol of Seville's willingness to embrace change and to honor its rich history while embracing a bold future. It stands as a reminder that buildings aren't just functional structures; they are expressions of a city's identity, narratives of evolution, and invitations to explore new horizons.

Dreamers and admirers of modern aesthetics, let the Metropol Parasol's intricate lattice and futuristic flair inspire your own quests for pushing boundaries. Just as it offers new perspectives on Seville, so too can your creations offer new perspectives on the spaces we inhabit. The Metropol Parasol's story whispers that every endeavor you embark upon, every project you invest in, can be a tribute to the spirit of innovation, the joy of exploration, and the celebration of harmonious integration between the modern and the traditional.

As you contemplate the Metropol Parasol's organic elegance against Seville's historic backdrop, remember that it's more than just a structure; it's a symbol of the city's commitment to progress, a testament to the fusion of creativity and functionality, and a reminder that the built environment can be a canvas for new narratives in the grand tapestry of history. Let its legacy encourage you to design not just for function, but for the elevation of aesthetics, the embrace of change, and the transformative power of imaginative design in shaping the cities of tomorrow.

56

Gateway Arch, USA

Imagine standing on the banks of the mighty Mississippi River, in the heart of St. Louis, USA, and gazing up at a monumental arc that seems to touch the sky – the Gateway Arch. This iconic structure isn't just a monument; it's a symbol of ambition and unity that invites us to envision the boundless possibilities of human endeavor, while marveling at the fusion of artistic vision and engineering brilliance.

Picture a time when a nation sought to honor its westward expansion and embrace its history of exploration, and the Gateway Arch emerged as a soaring tribute. Rising to prominence in the mid-20th century, this architectural marvel wasn't just a monument; it was a testament to the American spirit of adventure and discovery, a place where the past and the future converged in an awe-inspiring form. The Gateway Arch isn't just an edifice; it's a harmonious blend of symbolism, innovation, and the spirit of manifest destiny.

The Gateway Arch's design isn't just architecture; it's a marvel of engineering that stands as the tallest arch in the world. Its sleek, stainless steel form, towering over 600 feet, captures the essence of upward mobility and progress. The curvaceous lines of the arch evoke a sense of movement and aspiration, while the interior spaces offer a contemplative environment that encourages reflection and unity.

As you picture yourself looking up at the Gateway Arch's monumental curve and sense the enormity of human achievement, think of the architects who dared to dream on such a grand scale, the engineers who turned a vision into reality. The Gateway Arch isn't just a structure; it's a tribute to the power of collective vision, the ability to craft symbols that resonate across generations.

Yet, its significance extends far beyond its impressive form. The Gateway Arch isn't just a monument; it's a symbol of America's pioneering spirit and its commitment to unity and exploration. It stands as a reminder that monuments aren't just landmarks; they are stories etched in metal and stone that tell of a nation's courage, evolution, and quest for progress.

Dreamers and believers in the American dream, let the Gateway Arch's sweeping form and soaring symbolism inspire your own quests for reaching new heights. Just as it represents the pursuit of horizons, so too can your aspirations soar above limitations. The Gateway Arch's story whispers that every endeavor you embark upon, every project you invest in, can be a tribute to the power of vision, the pursuit of unity, and the celebration of human tenacity.

As you contemplate the Gateway Arch's elegant curve against St. Louis' urban landscape, remember that it's more than just a monument; it's a testament to America's determination, a symbol of progress, and a reminder that the human impulse to explore and evolve is as boundless as the sky. Let its legacy encourage you to design not just for aesthetics, but for the elevation of human potential, the embrace of diversity, and the transformative power of monumental ideas in the grand tapestry of history.

57

World Trade Center, USA

Imagine gazing at the Manhattan skyline, and amidst the bustling cityscape, a phoenix-like tower rises with resolute grace – the One World Trade Center. This iconic structure isn't just a skyscraper; it's a beacon of resilience and hope that invites us to witness the triumph of human spirit over adversity, while marveling at the fusion of architectural innovation and the indomitable strength of a nation.

Picture a time when a city reclaimed its skyline and a nation stood united against darkness, and the One World Trade Center emerged as a symbol of rebirth. Emerging in the 21st century, this architectural marvel wasn't just a tower; it was a testament to New York's unwavering spirit and the world's collective resolve to rise from the ashes. The One World Trade Center isn't just an edifice; it's a fusion of architectural brilliance, memorial, and the embodiment of resilience.

The One World Trade Center's design isn't just architecture; it's a masterpiece that channels both elegance and power. Its soaring height of over 1,700 feet is a tribute to aspiration and remembrance. The tower's base, with its museum and memorial, pays homage to the lives lost on September 11, 2001, while its sleek form pierces the sky, symbolizing hope, progress, and unity.

As you imagine yourself looking up at the One World Trade Center's gleaming façade, think of the architects who worked to craft a tower of both memory and progress, the engineers who turned determination into reality. The One World Trade Center isn't just a skyscraper; it's a living testament to the strength of human will, the ability to rise anew from the ashes of tragedy.

Yet, its significance extends far beyond its remarkable height. The One World Trade Center isn't just a building; it's a symbol of New York's resilience and the world's solidarity against terrorism. It stands as a reminder that towers aren't just structures; they are memorials, reflections of a city's resolve, and markers of history that teach us to honor the past while reaching for the future.

Dreamers and believers in the power of unity, let the One World Trade Center's symbolic ascent and unwavering presence inspire your own quests for overcoming challenges. Just as it stands tall amidst adversity, so too can your aspirations stand strong in the face of obstacles. The One World Trade Center's story whispers that every endeavor you embark upon, every project you invest in, can be a tribute to the human spirit's ability to rebuild, to remember, and to heal.

As you contemplate the One World Trade Center's dignified silhouette against New York's vibrant skyline, remember that it's more than just a tower; it's a testament to the city's heart, a symbol of global resilience, and a reminder that the human resolve to create, honor, and uplift is unyielding. Let its legacy encourage you to design not just for function, but for the elevation of shared values, the embrace of diversity, and the transformative power of rising anew in the grand tapestry of history.

58

Tower of David, Israel

Imagine standing before the ancient walls of Jerusalem, and amidst the layers of history, a towering sentinel rises with an air of timelessness – the Tower of David. This iconic structure isn't just a fortress; it's a storyteller of civilizations, a living witness to the passage of time that invites us to delve into the tapestry of human history, while marveling at the resilience of architectural heritage.

Picture a time when kings and conquerors shaped the destinies of empires, and the Tower of David emerged as a stronghold of power and symbolism. Rooted in the ancient world, this architectural marvel wasn't just a fortress; it was a sentinel of Jerusalem's past and a monument to the enduring spirit of the city. The Tower of David isn't just an edifice; it's a testament to the layers of culture, faith, and history that intertwine to create a living mosaic.

The Tower of David's design isn't just architecture; it's a testament to the fusion of cultures and the passage of time. Its stone walls, built by various rulers across centuries, embody a blend of Roman, Byzantine, and Islamic influences. The tower's battlements and turrets stand as guardians of memory, overlooking the city that has witnessed countless stories and upheavals.

As you imagine yourself walking through the Tower of David's ancient halls, think of the artisans and architects who worked across eras to shape a monument that transcends dynasties. The Tower of David isn't just a fortress; it's a living history book, a testament to human perseverance in the face of change and conflict.

Yet, its significance transcends its architectural grandeur. The Tower of David isn't just a structure; it's a symbol of Jerusalem's status as a spiritual crossroads and a center of civilization. It stands as a reminder that walls aren't just barriers; they are storytellers, guardians of the past, and reminders of the ongoing evolution of a city's identity.

Dreamers and lovers of history, let the Tower of David's ancient stones and enduring presence inspire your own quests for understanding and embracing the narratives of the past. Just as it stands as a guardian of history, so too can your creations stand as tributes to the stories that shape us. The

Tower of David's story whispers that every endeavor you embark upon, every project you invest in, can be a tribute to the threads of history, the power of remembrance, and the celebration of cultural heritage.

As you contemplate the Tower of David's commanding presence against Jerusalem's sacred skyline, remember that it's more than just a fortress; it's a living witness, a symbol of resilience, and a reminder that the stories of the past continue to shape the narratives of the present. Let its legacy encourage you to design not just for beauty, but for the elevation of human connection, the embrace of diversity, and the transformative power of embracing history in the grand tapestry of time.

59

Alcatraz Island, USA

Imagine an island emerging from the waters of San Francisco Bay, shrouded in mist and mystery – Alcatraz Island. This iconic place isn't just an island; it's a fortress of isolation and redemption, a canvas that invites us to explore the narratives of confinement and escape, while marveling at the intricate dance of nature and human determination, all set against the backdrop of a unique and storied architecture.

ALCATRAZ ISLAND, USA

Picture a time when Alcatraz was more than just an island; it was a maximum-security prison, known as "The Rock." Rooted in history, this place wasn't just a prison; it was a crucible of human stories, a realm where infamous criminals lived side by side with the dream of freedom. Alcatraz Island isn't just a landmass; it's a testimony to the complexity of human behavior, the struggle for justice, and the potential for transformation.

Alcatraz's design isn't just architecture; it's a testament to adapting nature to serve human needs. The imposing cellblocks and watchtowers stand in stark contrast to the island's natural beauty, serving as a reminder of the confinement within. Yet, the prison's isolation also allowed nature to reclaim parts of the island, creating a unique ecosystem that thrives against the odds.

As you imagine yourself walking through the dimly lit cellblocks, think of the prisoners who dreamed of freedom and the guards who maintained order in this unforgiving environment. Alcatraz Island isn't just a place; it's a microcosm of human struggle, a living testament to the complexities of justice and rehabilitation.

Yet, its significance extends beyond its prison walls. Alcatraz Island isn't just a rock; it's a symbol of resilience, a marker of historical shifts, and a lens through which we examine society's approach to crime and punishment. It stands as a reminder that islands aren't just geographical features; they can be islands of transformation, places where we confront our past and seek paths toward a better future.

Dreamers and believers in redemption, let Alcatraz's stories of captivity and escape inspire your own quests for personal growth and societal change. Just as it stands as a symbol of both isolation and hope, so too can your endeavors inspire transformation and rehabilitation. Alcatraz Island's story whispers that every endeavor you embark upon, every project you invest in, can be a tribute to the complexities of human nature, the power of second chances, and the celebration of resilience.

As you contemplate Alcatraz Island's stark silhouette against the sweeping expanse of San Francisco Bay, remember that it's more than just a prison; it's a reminder of the human capacity for change, a symbol of justice and renewal, and a beacon that challenges us to seek transformation amidst challenges. Let its legacy encourage you to design not just for utility, but for the elevation of human potential, the embrace of history's lessons, and the transformative power of striving for a better society in the grand tapestry of humanity's journey.

60

Blue Mosque, Turkey

Imagine standing at the crossroads of history and spirituality, in the heart of Istanbul, where a majestic silhouette rises against the sky – the Blue

Mosque. This iconic structure isn't just a mosque; it's a symphony of faith and artistry, an embodiment of devotion that invites us to delve into the essence of Islamic architecture and cultural synthesis, all while marveling at the serene elegance that defines its unique beauty.

Picture a time when the Ottoman Empire flourished, and Sultan Ahmet I dreamt of a mosque that would reflect the grandeur of his reign. Rooted in the past, this architectural marvel wasn't just a mosque; it was a testament to the Sultan's vision, an aspiration to create a masterpiece that would stand as a tribute to both human devotion and artistic excellence. The Blue Mosque isn't just a building; it's a living manifestation of the harmony between faith and creativity.

The Blue Mosque's design isn't just architecture; it's a marriage of Islamic and Byzantine influences. Its cascading domes, cascading domes, and six minarets pay homage to Ottoman tradition, while the exquisite blue tiles that adorn its interior walls give the mosque its evocative name. The intricate patterns and harmonious proportions of the mosque offer a sense of tranquility that resonates with the essence of Islamic philosophy.

As you imagine yourself stepping into the Blue Mosque's hallowed halls, think of the artisans who meticulously handcrafted the tiles, the architects who envisioned a sanctuary that would inspire spiritual contemplation. The Blue Mosque isn't just a place of worship; it's a labor of love, a masterpiece that transcends time and place.

Yet, its significance goes beyond its architectural beauty. The Blue Mosque isn't just a mosque; it's a symbol of unity, a reflection of Istanbul's rich history as a crossroads of cultures, where East and West converged. It stands as a reminder that mosques aren't just places of prayer; they are bridges that connect us to the divine and to one another, embodying the values of community and reverence.

Dreamers and admirers of beauty, let the Blue Mosque's serene ambiance and intricate designs inspire your own quests for artistic expression and spiritual connection. Just as it harmonizes aesthetics and devotion, so too can your endeavors harmonize creativity and purpose. The Blue Mosque's story whispers that every endeavor you embark upon, every project you invest in, can be a testament to the marriage of beauty and meaning, the power of unity, and the celebration of diverse cultural legacies.

As you contemplate the Blue Mosque's timeless allure against the backdrop of Istanbul's bustling cityscape, remember that it's more than just a mosque; it's a masterpiece of human endeavor, a beacon of harmony, and a sanctuary that reminds us of the eternal pursuit of the divine. Let its legacy encourage you to design not just for aesthetics, but for the elevation of the human spirit, the embrace of cultural synthesis, and the transformative power of faith in the grand tapestry of existence.

61

Sydney Tower Eye, Australia

Imagine standing in the heart of Sydney, gazing up at the sky-piercing marvel that is the Sydney Tower Eye. This iconic structure isn't just a tower; it's a soaring tribute to human ingenuity, an invitation to explore the city from breathtaking heights, while marveling at the fusion of modern design and urban fascination.

Picture a time when Sydney was evolving into a bustling metropolis, with a desire to showcase its cosmopolitan charm. Rooted in recent history, this architectural marvel wasn't just a tower; it was a symbol of Sydney's ambition, a testament to its evolution from colonial outpost to a global city that stands tall on the world stage. The Sydney Tower Eye isn't just an observation deck; it's a testament to the city's dynamism and progress.

The Sydney Tower Eye's design isn't just architecture; it's an engineering marvel. Its towering spire and sleek, futuristic design capture the essence of modernity while offering a panoramic view of the city and its stunning surroundings. The glass-floored Skywalk and rotating dining experience redefine the traditional concept of an observation deck, elevating it to an immersive journey of sight and sensation.

As you imagine yourself stepping onto the Sydney Tower Eye's observation deck, think of the architects and engineers who harnessed technology to create an unparalleled experience. The Sydney Tower Eye isn't just an attraction; it's a testament to human curiosity and the unending quest to reach new heights, both literally and metaphorically.

Yet, its significance goes beyond its impressive design. The Sydney Tower Eye isn't just a tower; it's a symbol of Sydney's aspiration to offer a unique perspective on the world, a reflection of the city's commitment to innovation and inclusivity. It stands as a reminder that towers aren't just landmarks; they are gateways that inspire us to see things differently, to transcend our limits, and to experience life from new angles.

Dreamers and seekers of inspiration, let the Sydney Tower Eye's panoramic views and modern aesthetics inspire your own quests for innovative thinking and fresh perspectives. Just as it offers a new way of looking at Sydney, so too can your endeavors offer fresh viewpoints and creative solutions. The

Sydney Tower Eye's story whispers that every endeavor you embark upon, every project you invest in, can be a tribute to the spirit of exploration, the power of forward thinking, and the celebration of human potential.

As you contemplate the Sydney Tower Eye's striking presence against the backdrop of Sydney's vibrant cityscape, remember that it's more than just a tower; it's a testament to progress, a symbol of embracing the future, and a platform that encourages us to reach for the skies – both in the realm of architecture and in the pursuit of our dreams. Let its legacy encourage you to design not just for functionality, but for the elevation of possibilities, the embrace of innovation, and the transformative power of aspiration in the grand tapestry of human achievement.

62

Paul's Cathedral, UK

Imagine strolling through the bustling streets of London, when suddenly, a majestic sight emerges – St. Paul's Cathedral. This iconic structure isn't just a cathedral; it's a beacon of resilience and spiritual solace, an invitation to marvel at the fusion of artistic brilliance and historical significance, while immersing yourself in the grandeur of British history.

Picture a time when London was rebuilding after the devastating Great Fire of 1666, when Sir Christopher Wren envisioned a cathedral that would symbolize the city's rebirth. Rooted in the past, this architectural marvel wasn't just a place of worship; it was a testament to human perseverance, an embodiment of the city's determination to rise from the ashes stronger than ever. St. Paul's Cathedral isn't just a building; it's a testament to the human spirit's capacity to rebuild and renew.

St. Paul's Cathedral's design isn't just architecture; it's a masterpiece of Baroque style. Its grand dome and elegant facade are a testament to Sir Christopher Wren's innovative approach, seamlessly blending classical influences with contemporary vision. The Whispering Gallery, an acoustic marvel, allows even a whisper to travel across the dome's expanse, demonstrating the cathedral's embrace of both artistic beauty and scientific marvels.

As you imagine yourself ascending the steps of St. Paul's Cathedral, think of the craftsmen who painstakingly carved its intricate details, the visionaries who designed its soaring dome, and the generations who have sought solace within its walls. St. Paul's Cathedral isn't just a place of worship; it's a testament to human creativity, a living canvas that tells the story of London's resilience and the legacy of its architects.

Yet, its significance extends beyond its architectural splendor. St. Paul's Cathedral isn't just a cathedral; it's a symbol of unity, a reflection of London's enduring spirit during times of crisis, and a cultural touchstone that spans centuries. It stands as a reminder that cathedrals aren't just religious sites; they are landmarks that connect us to history, spirituality, and the essence of a nation.

Dreamers and admirers of history, let St. Paul's Cathedral's timeless beauty and historical narrative inspire your own quests for purpose and creative expression. Just as it stands as a monument to renewal, so too can your endeavors embody the resilience of the human spirit. St. Paul's Cathedral's story whispers that every endeavor you embark upon, every project you invest in, can be a tribute to the strength of determination, the power of heritage, and the celebration of cultural heritage.

As you contemplate St. Paul's Cathedral's majestic dome against the backdrop of London's bustling urban landscape, remember that it's more than just a cathedral; it's a testament to rebirth, a symbol of endurance, and a sanctuary that calls us to find meaning amidst challenges. Let its legacy encourage you to design not just for aesthetics, but for the elevation of human potential, the embrace of history's lessons, and the transformative power of faith in the grand tapestry of existence.

63

Palace of Culture and Science, Poland

Imagine entering the heart of Warsaw, Poland, and being greeted by a towering masterpiece that seems to touch the sky – the Palace of Culture and Science. This iconic structure isn't just a building; it's a testament to human aspiration, an invitation to explore a blend of historical significance and innovative design, while marveling at its towering presence against the cityscape.

Picture a time when Poland was emerging from the shadows of World War II, and the country sought to rebuild and redefine itself. Rooted in history, this architectural marvel wasn't just a palace; it was a gift from the Soviet Union, a symbol of cultural exchange and cooperation. The Palace of Culture and Science isn't just a building; it's a living reminder of a pivotal era in Poland's journey toward modernization.

The Palace of Culture and Science's design isn't just architecture; it's a fusion of Socialist Realism and modernist influences. Its towering spire and ornate details reflect the aesthetics of the era, while its size and scope were a testament to the ambition of the time. The innovative use of space, including theaters, museums, and offices, showcased a forward-thinking approach to urban planning.

As you imagine yourself standing beneath the Palace's grand entrance, think of the architects and laborers who dedicated themselves to its construction, the generations who have walked its halls, and the city it has watched over for decades. The Palace of Culture and Science isn't just a building; it's a witness to history, a symbol of Poland's journey toward identity and modernity.

Yet, its significance goes beyond its architectural grandeur. The Palace of Culture and Science isn't just a palace; it's a symbol of resilience, a reflection of Poland's complex history of political and cultural shifts, and a venue that has hosted countless events that shaped the nation's narrative. It stands as a reminder that buildings aren't just structures; they are witnesses to the evolution of society, markers of progress and transformation.

Dreamers and seekers of identity, let the Palace of Culture and Science's monumental presence and historical narrative inspire your own quests for self-discovery and creative expression. Just as it stands as a witness to change, so too can your endeavors become milestones in your personal journey. The Palace of Culture and Science's story whispers that every endeavor you embark upon, every project you invest in, can be a tribute to the spirit of transformation, the power of collaboration, and the celebration of cultural legacy.

As you contemplate the Palace's towering silhouette against the backdrop of Warsaw's bustling streets, remember that it's more than just a palace; it's a symbol of progress, a guardian of memory, and a space that echoes with the voices of generations. Let its legacy encourage you to design not just for aesthetics, but for the elevation of cultural identity, the embrace of history's lessons, and the transformative power of unity in the grand tapestry of human experience.

64

Lotte World Tower, South Korea

Imagine being in the heart of Seoul, South Korea, and gazing up in awe at a towering wonder that seems to connect earth and sky – the Lotte World Tower. This iconic structure isn't just a skyscraper; it's a testament to human imagination, an invitation to witness the fusion of modern technology and artistic ingenuity, all while marveling at its breathtaking presence against the city's skyline.

Picture a time when Seoul was embracing the future with fervor, and the city sought to make a mark on the world stage. Rooted in recent history, this architectural marvel wasn't just a tower; it was a symbol of South Korea's economic and cultural ascent, a reflection of the nation's determination to carve out its place in the global narrative. The Lotte World Tower isn't just a building; it's a beacon of ambition and progress.

The Lotte World Tower's design isn't just architecture; it's a masterpiece of innovation. Its sleek and slender form, inspired by traditional Korean artistry, rises with grace and grandeur, adorned with intricate details that pay homage to the country's heritage. The use of cutting-edge technology in its construction and the inclusion of sustainable features showcase a commitment to both modernity and environmental responsibility.

As you imagine yourself standing at the foot of the Lotte World Tower, think of the engineers who defied gravity to bring this vision to life, the architects who harmonized tradition and modernity, and the countless individuals who contributed to its creation. The Lotte World Tower isn't just a skyscraper; it's a testament to human potential, a tangible representation of what can be achieved when dreams are nurtured with dedication.

Yet, its significance extends beyond its towering presence. The Lotte World Tower isn't just a skyscraper; it's a symbol of South Korea's emergence as a global player, a reflection of the nation's fusion of tradition and progress, and a landmark that stands as a testament to its cultural identity. It stands as a reminder that buildings aren't just structures; they are mirrors that reflect a nation's aspirations, its ideals, and its evolution.

Dreamers and believers in possibility, let the Lotte World Tower's soaring height and intricate design inspire your own quests for innovation and self-discovery. Just as it reaches for the sky, so too can your endeavors reach new heights of creativity and accomplishment. The Lotte World Tower's story whispers that every endeavor you embark upon, every project you invest in, can be a tribute to the boundless power of human imagination, the spirit of progress, and the celebration of cultural heritage.

As you contemplate the Lotte World Tower's elegant silhouette against Seoul's vibrant cityscape, remember that it's more than just a skyscraper; it's a symbol of aspiration, a guardian of dreams, and a monument that testifies to the potency of perseverance. Let its legacy encourage you to design not just for functionality, but for the elevation of human potential, the embrace of innovation, and the transformative power of vision in the grand tapestry of human achievement.

65

Montparnasse Tower, France

Imagine yourself in the heart of Paris, where a unique and modern wonder rises against the backdrop of timeless beauty – the Montparnasse Tower. This iconic structure isn't just a skyscraper; it's a testament to boldness, an invitation to see the city in a new light, and an opportunity to embrace the harmonious coexistence of tradition and innovation.

Picture a time when Paris was evolving, and the city sought to make a statement about its future. Rooted in recent history, this architectural marvel wasn't just a tower; it was a response to the city's changing urban landscape, a symbol of Paris's willingness to embrace modernity while safeguarding its cherished heritage. The Montparnasse Tower isn't just a building; it's a declaration of Paris's commitment to progress.

The Montparnasse Tower's design isn't just architecture; it's a daring departure from convention. Its sleek and minimalistic silhouette, a stark contrast to the historic charm of Paris, represents a bold step into the future. The innovative use of materials and technology in its construction showcases an avant-garde approach that invites visitors to experience Paris from a fresh perspective.

As you imagine yourself standing at the base of the Montparnasse Tower, think of the architects who dared to challenge the status quo, the visionaries who saw beyond tradition, and the pioneers who turned a vertical canvas into an urban icon. The Montparnasse Tower isn't just a skyscraper; it's a tribute to human courage, a testament to the power of envisioning the extraordinary.

Yet, its significance goes beyond its towering presence. The Montparnasse Tower isn't just a skyscraper; it's a symbol of evolution, a reflection of Paris's dynamic spirit, and a landmark that prompts us to reflect on the dynamic relationship between the old and the new. It stands as a reminder that buildings aren't just structures; they are statements that cities make about their essence and their trajectory.

Dreamers and adventurers, let the Montparnasse Tower's modernity and audacity inspire your own quests for innovation and authenticity. Just as it defies convention, so too can your endeavors challenge the norms and explore uncharted territories. The Montparnasse Tower's story whispers that every endeavor you embark upon, every project you invest in, can be a celebration of individuality, the pursuit of progress, and the recognition of the beauty that emerges when contrasts collide.

As you contemplate the Montparnasse Tower's distinctive outline against the romantic tapestry of Paris, remember that it's more than just a skyscraper; it's a symbol of courage, a mirror of the changing times, and a monument that testifies to the vitality of transformation. Let its legacy encourage you to design not just for aesthetics, but for the elevation of innovation, the embrace of change, and the transformative power of embracing the new in the grand tapestry of human achievement.

66

International Commerce Centre, Hong Kong

Imagine standing at the vibrant heart of Hong Kong, where a marvel of modern engineering and ambition reaches towards the heavens – the International Commerce Centre (ICC). This iconic structure isn't just a skyscraper; it's a symbol of Hong Kong's unwavering spirit, an invitation to witness the blend of innovation and global connectivity, and a chance to be inspired by human achievement against the backdrop of a bustling metropolis.

Picture a time when Hong Kong was embracing its role as an international financial hub, seeking to create an architectural masterpiece that would reflect its global prominence. Rooted in recent history, this architectural marvel wasn't just a building; it was a testament to Hong Kong's status as a world leader in finance and trade, a beacon that shines across continents. The International Commerce Centre isn't just a tower; it's a testament to Hong Kong's influence on the world stage.

The International Commerce Centre's design isn't just architecture; it's a fusion of form and function. Its sleek and modern facade, punctuated by crystalline elements, rises with elegance and sophistication. The innovative use of cutting-edge technology in its construction, as well as its sustainability features, showcases a commitment to both modernity and responsible development.

As you imagine yourself standing beneath the towering height of the International Commerce Centre, think of the architects who envisioned the future, the engineers who turned blueprints into reality, and the dreamers who saw a vision of Hong Kong that transcended boundaries. The International Commerce Centre isn't just a skyscraper; it's a tribute to human ingenuity, a testament to the power of turning aspirations into reality.

Yet, its significance extends beyond its architectural splendor. The International Commerce Centre isn't just a skyscraper; it's a symbol of Hong Kong's resilience, a reflection of the city's global connectivity, and a landmark that stands as a testament to its ability to adapt and thrive in a rapidly changing world. It stands as a reminder that buildings aren't just structures; they are mirrors that reflect a city's dynamism, its place in the global narrative, and its role in shaping the future.

Dreamers and visionaries, let the International Commerce Centre's towering height and innovative design inspire your own quests for excellence and global impact. Just as it touches the sky, so too can your endeavors reach new heights of innovation and influence. The International Commerce Centre's story whispers that every endeavor you embark upon, every project you invest in, can be a celebration of ambition, the pursuit of excellence, and the recognition that the sky is not the limit, but the beginning.

As you contemplate the International Commerce Centre's gleaming facade against the backdrop of Hong Kong's bustling energy, remember that it's more than just a skyscraper; it's a symbol of aspiration, a beacon of global connectivity, and a testament to the resilience of a city that thrives on change. Let its legacy encourage you to design not just for aesthetics, but for the elevation of human potential, the embrace of innovation, and the transformative power of dreams in the grand tapestry of human achievement.

67

Tokyo Skytree, Japan

Picture yourself in the heart of Tokyo, where the bustling energy of a modern metropolis meets the tranquility of traditional Japanese culture, and rising proudly amidst it all is the Tokyo Skytree. This iconic structure isn't just a tower; it's a reflection of Japan's harmony between past and present, an

TOKYO SKYTREE, JAPAN

invitation to embrace technological marvels while cherishing ancient values, and a chance to witness the power of innovation against the backdrop of a city that seamlessly blends old and new.

Imagine a time when Tokyo was seeking to build a beacon of modernity that would honor its rich heritage. Rooted in recent history, this architectural marvel wasn't just a structure; it was a tribute to Tokyo's rise as a global hub of innovation, a testament to its ability to honor tradition while pushing the boundaries of design and engineering. The Tokyo Skytree isn't just a tower; it's a declaration of Tokyo's commitment to honor the past while embracing the future.

The Tokyo Skytree's design isn't just architecture; it's a fusion of Japan's aesthetic principles and cutting-edge engineering that reaches for the heavens. Its elegant form, inspired by traditional pagodas and Japan's appreciation for simplicity, rises with grace and precision. The innovative use of advanced materials, earthquake-resistant features, and eco-friendly elements showcases a commitment to both heritage and technological progress.

As you imagine yourself standing beneath the towering height of the Tokyo Skytree, think of the architects who harmonized tradition and innovation, the engineers who transformed dreams into reality, and the visionaries who saw Tokyo's potential to be a global leader in design. The Tokyo Skytree isn't just a tower; it's a testament to human collaboration, a symbol of creativity's power, and the embodiment of the belief that cities evolve by embracing both their roots and their aspirations.

However, its significance transcends its impressive stature. The Tokyo Skytree isn't just a tower; it's a symbol of Tokyo's resilience, a reflection of the city's reverence for its past, and a monument that invites people from around the world to witness the synthesis of modernity and tradition. It stands as a reminder that buildings aren't just structures; they are cultural expressions that tell stories, define cities, and connect generations.

Dreamers and admirers of beauty, let the Tokyo Skytree's soaring heights and fusion of tradition and innovation inspire your own quests for excellence and cultural understanding. Just as it bridges the gap between ancient and contemporary, so too can your endeavors transcend boundaries and bring different worlds together. The Tokyo Skytree's story whispers that every endeavor you embark upon, every project you nurture, can be a celebration of human potential, a testament to cultural respect, and a reminder that progress is a journey of balance.

As you contemplate the Tokyo Skytree's elegant form against Tokyo's vibrant backdrop, remember that it's more than just a tower; it's a symbol of aspiration, an emblem of cultural synthesis, and a monument to the idea that greatness is achieved when technology and tradition harmonize. Let its legacy encourage you to design not just for aesthetics, but for the elevation of cultural appreciation, the embrace of innovation, and the transformative power of finding unity in diversity in the grand tapestry of human achievement.

68

The Great Sphinx of Giza, Egypt

Close your eyes and travel back in time to ancient Egypt, where the sands of the desert hold secrets of a civilization that shaped the course of history. Amidst the breathtaking expanse of the Giza Plateau emerges a mystical guardian that has stood the test of time – the Great Sphinx of Giza. This iconic monument isn't just a statue; it's a sentinel of eternity, a symbol of wisdom and mystery, and a window into a world that existed millennia ago.

Imagine a time when pharaohs ruled the Nile, pyramids pierced the skies, and the land was imbued with the magic of legends. Rooted in the distant past, the Great Sphinx wasn't just a carving; it was a tribute to Egypt's spiritual beliefs, a testament to its advanced engineering, and a guardian that watched over the pyramids with an air of enigmatic wisdom. The Great Sphinx isn't just a sculpture; it's a legacy of Egypt's mastery over art, culture, and architecture.

The Great Sphinx's design isn't just a stone figure; it's a fusion of human and lion, a symbol of strength and intellect intertwined. Its unique form, with the body of a regal lion and the face of a wise pharaoh, is a testament to Egypt's fascination with duality and its veneration of royalty. The innovative use of massive limestone blocks and precision carving showcases an ancient civilization's ability to mold nature into art.

As you imagine yourself standing before the majestic Great Sphinx, think of the artisans who chiseled every detail, the engineers who sculpted stone with remarkable precision, and the thinkers who wove spirituality into art. The Great Sphinx isn't just a statue; it's a tribute to human ingenuity, a testament to craftsmanship's ability to transcend time, and the embodiment of the belief that art has the power to connect generations.

Yet, its significance transcends its awe-inspiring presence. The Great Sphinx isn't just a statue; it's a symbol of Egypt's cultural legacy, a relic of a society's deep reverence for both deities and rulers, and a monument that beckons travelers from across the globe to touch the past. It stands as a reminder that monuments aren't just stone and mortar; they are fragments of a civilization's story, etched into the landscape to inspire wonder and curiosity.

Dreamers and seekers of wisdom, let the Great Sphinx's timeless gaze and enigmatic aura inspire your own quests for knowledge and discovery. Just as it has witnessed countless sunrises and sunsets, so too can your endeavors leave lasting imprints on the sands of time. The Great Sphinx's story whispers that every pursuit you undertake, every inquiry you make, can be a celebration of human curiosity, a testament to the quest for understanding, and a reminder that even across the ages, humanity's quest for meaning persists.

As you contemplate the Great Sphinx's serene countenance against Egypt's ancient backdrop, remember that it's more than just a statue; it's a symbol of Egypt's heritage, an emblem of mystery, and a monument to the idea that human hands can craft works that endure beyond epochs. Let its legacy inspire you to design not just for the present, but for the elevation of knowledge, the embrace of culture, and the transformative power of preserving the past in the grand tapestry of human achievement.

69

Moai Statues, Easter Island

Imagine a remote island in the vast Pacific Ocean, shrouded in mystery and brimming with enigmatic statues that defy time and distance – Easter Island, home to the remarkable Moai statues. These iconic figures aren't merely stone sculptures; they are guardians of a lost world, symbols of ancestral connection, and an embodiment of the human spirit's ability to create and endure against all odds.

Travel back in time to a place where nature and culture converged, and a people flourished in isolation. Rooted in the island's history, the Moai statues weren't just rock formations; they were a testament to the Rapa Nui's reverence for their ancestors, a tribute to their craftsmanship, and a way to connect the past with the present. The Moai statues aren't just monoliths; they are echoes of a society's beliefs, a reflection of its identity, and a testament to the resilience of human creativity.

The Moai's design isn't just sculpture; it's a harmonious blend of spirituality and skill, shaped by the hands of artists who drew inspiration from their surroundings. The towering forms, with elongated bodies and distinctive features, carry an air of stoic nobility. The innovative technique of carving massive stones, transporting them across the island, and erecting them on ceremonial platforms showcases the Rapa Nui's remarkable engineering prowess.

As you imagine yourself standing before the silent guardians of Easter Island, think of the hands that carved these figures, the minds that infused them with meaning, and the hearts that valued ancestral connection. The Moai statues aren't just sculptures; they are a testament to human creativity, a bridge across generations, and a reminder that art transcends time and space.

However, their significance isn't confined to their island home. The Moai statues aren't just sculptures; they are symbols of human ingenuity, a reflection of cultural identity, and a reminder that the past shapes the present. They stand as a testament that monuments aren't just symbols; they are cultural artifacts that invite us to contemplate the interplay of art, history, and humanity.

Dreamers and seekers of heritage, let the Moai's silent gazes and steadfast presence inspire your own quests for connection and preservation. Just as they stand strong against the elements, so too can your endeavors withstand challenges and preserve the essence of what makes us human. The Moai's story whispers that every endeavor you embark upon, every effort to connect the threads of culture, can be a celebration of ancestral wisdom, a testament to the value of heritage, and a reminder that the past's echoes shape our future.

As you contemplate the Moai's solemn forms against the backdrop of Easter Island's beauty, remember that they're more than just statues; they're a symbol of cultural pride, an emblem of connection, and a testament to the idea that humanity's legacy is etched in stone and spirit. Let their legacy inspire you to design not just for aesthetics, but for the elevation of tradition, the embrace of diversity, and the transformative power of honoring our roots in the grand tapestry of human achievement.

70

Cappadocia Cave Churches, Turkey

Imagine a land where rocky landscapes and ancient faiths intertwine to create a realm of wonder – Cappadocia, Turkey. In this captivating region, the earth itself becomes a canvas for spiritual expression through the awe-inspiring Cappadocia Cave Churches. These remarkable structures aren't just places of worship; they are sanctuaries carved into stone, where spirituality and innovation meld to form a testament to human devotion and creativity.

Travel back in time to a period when people sought solace in nature's embrace and carved homes in the soft rock. Rooted in history, the Cappadocia Cave Churches weren't just places of prayer; they were a reflection of the Byzantine era's religious fervor, a canvas for artistic expression, and a sanctuary where faith found a harmonious dwelling. The Cappadocia Cave Churches aren't just caves; they are echoes of devotion, a testament to architecture's ability to mold nature, and a celebration of the sacred.

The design of the Cappadocia Cave Churches isn't just architecture; it's a harmonious blend of earthly and divine elements, shaped by the hands of artisans who carved rock with reverence. The interiors are adorned with exquisite frescoes that narrate stories of faith and life, while the natural surroundings offer a serene atmosphere for reflection. The innovative use of rock as both building material and canvas showcases humanity's ability to transform the ordinary into the extraordinary.

As you imagine yourself stepping into the cool embrace of the Cappadocia Cave Churches, think of the artists who adorned these cavernous walls, the architects who harnessed nature's formations, and the believers who sought communion within these sacred spaces. The Cappadocia Cave Churches aren't just architectural wonders; they are a testament to human devotion, a bridge between the physical and spiritual worlds, and a reminder that art and faith can intertwine to create breathtaking masterpieces.

Their significance resonates beyond their rock-hewn walls. The Cappadocia Cave Churches aren't just structures; they are symbols of cultural heritage, an embodiment of faith's enduring power, and a reminder that history's brushstrokes shape our understanding of the past. They stand as a testament that monuments aren't just buildings; they are conduits of spiritual insight, places where past and present meet, and reminders that humanity's spiritual journey transcends time.

Dreamers and seekers of wisdom, let the Cappadocia Cave Churches' serene beauty and spiritual aura inspire your own quests for meaning and connection. Just as these ancient sanctuaries bear the weight of centuries, so too can your endeavors carry the legacy of cultural preservation and spiritual enrichment. The Cappadocia Cave Churches' story whispers that every endeavor you embark upon, every step you take in the realm of creativity and faith, can be a celebration of humanity's spiritual yearning, a testament to the fusion of art and devotion, and a reminder that the sacred is present in the grand tapestry of human achievement.

As you contemplate the Cappadocia Cave Churches' intricate frescoes against the backdrop of nature's splendor, remember that they are more than just caves; they are an embodiment of spiritual resilience, an emblem of cultural heritage, and a testament to the idea that humanity's quest for the divine is etched into both the rock and the soul. Let their legacy inspire you to design not just for the eye, but for the elevation of the spirit, the embrace of tradition, and the transformative power of sacred spaces in the grand tapestry of human achievement.

71

Trevi Fountain, Italy

Picture a scene straight out of a dream, where wishes are whispered into the glistening waters, and art dances amidst the Roman air – the Trevi Fountain in Italy. This enchanting masterpiece isn't just a fountain; it's a symphony of water and stone, a beacon of romance, and a testament to humanity's eternal connection to beauty and dreams.

Imagine strolling through the cobbled streets of Rome, where the sound of rushing water guides you to a marvel that has captured hearts for centuries. The Trevi Fountain isn't just a monument; it's a celebration of the city's history, a nod to its ancient aqueducts, and a nod to the Roman gods of the sea. The Trevi Fountain isn't just a sculpture; it's a place where wishes are whispered, where travelers pause to marvel, and where artists find inspiration.

The design of the Trevi Fountain isn't just architecture; it's a delicate dance of sculpture and water, a fusion of Baroque exuberance and classical grace. The central figure of Oceanus, astride his chariot, embodies the power and vastness of the sea. The intricate details of seashells, tritons, and horses evoke a sense of movement frozen in time. The innovative use of perspective and space makes it seem as if the figures are emerging from the stone and water itself.

Close your eyes and imagine standing before the Trevi Fountain, tossing a coin over your shoulder into the clear water, joining the countless others who've done the same. Think of the artists who chiseled these stones, the dreamers who made their wishes, and the generations who've been touched by its magic. The Trevi Fountain isn't just a landmark; it's a testament to human aspirations, a connection to the past, and a reminder that art can shape both the physical world and our deepest desires.

However, its significance extends beyond its artistic beauty. The Trevi Fountain isn't just a fountain; it's a symbol of romance, an emblem of cultural legacy, and a reminder that even in a world of concrete and steel, our yearning for beauty and connection remains timeless. It stands as a testament that monuments aren't just structures; they are repositories of collective dreams, places where art and architecture become vessels for our innermost hopes.

Dreamers and wanderers, let the Trevi Fountain's timeless charm and shimmering waters inspire your own quests for beauty and fulfillment. Just as the water flows ceaselessly, so too can your aspirations surge towards your dreams. The Trevi Fountain's story whispers that every coin you toss, every wish you make, can be a celebration of human imagination, a testament to the universal language of art, and a reminder that in the simplest of moments, the profound and the magical coalesce.

As you gaze at the Trevi Fountain's ethereal glow beneath the Roman sun, remember that it's more than just a fountain; it's an embodiment of cultural heritage, an emblem of artistic enchantment, and a testament to the idea that our thirst for beauty and our yearning for connection are etched into both our hearts and the fabric of the world. Let its legacy inspire you to design not just for function, but for the elevation of the human spirit, the celebration of dreams, and the transformative power of architectural wonders in the grand tapestry of human achievement.

72

Victoria Falls Bridge, Zambia/Zimbabwe

Imagine a breathtaking tapestry of nature and engineering that spans a chasm of roaring waters, connecting two nations – the Victoria Falls Bridge. This magnificent structure isn't just a bridge; it's a testament to human ingenuity harmonizing with the grandeur of the natural world, a symbol of unity across borders, and a reminder that architecture can be a bridge not only of steel and stone but of nations and cultures.

Close your eyes and picture the awe-inspiring Victoria Falls, where the Zambezi River plunges into the abyss, creating a deafening symphony of water and mist. Now, envision a remarkable feat of engineering, a bridge that spans the chasm with grace. The Victoria Falls Bridge isn't just a crossing; it's a link between Zambia and Zimbabwe, a marvel of late 19th-century design, and a connection between two nations sharing the majestic beauty of the falls.

The design of the Victoria Falls Bridge isn't just architecture; it's a fusion of utilitarian engineering and artistic vision. Designed by George Imbault and built under the guidance of Sir Cecil Rhodes, it stands as a tribute to the daring spirit of exploration and progress of its time. The iron lattice trusses rise from the rocky terrain, allowing trains to traverse the gorge with a view of the falls unparalleled in its majesty.

Imagine standing on the bridge, feeling the vibrations of the trains passing beneath you and witnessing the breathtaking cascade of Victoria Falls. Think of the laborers who toiled to build it, the engineers who conceived it, and the generations who've walked its expanse. The Victoria Falls Bridge isn't just a structure; it's a portal to adventure, a reminder of human ambition, and a celebration of the bond between nature and civilization.

However, its significance extends beyond its functional purpose. The Victoria Falls Bridge isn't just a bridge; it's a symbol of connection, an emblem of exploration, and a testament to the potential of collaboration across borders. It stands as a reminder that bridges can not only span physical divides but also foster cultural exchange, economic growth, and the understanding that transcends boundaries.

Imagine travelers from different corners of the world, standing together on the Victoria Falls Bridge, captivated by the natural wonder beneath their feet. Imagine their shared sense of awe, reminding us that no matter where we come from, the beauty of the natural world and the achievements of human endeavor are universal languages.

Dreamers and adventurers, let the Victoria Falls Bridge's harmonious blend of nature and engineering inspire your own journeys of collaboration and connection. Just as this bridge unites nations, so too can your ideas unite communities, cultures, and aspirations. The Victoria Falls Bridge's story whispers that every collaboration, every connection, can be a tribute to the human spirit, a celebration of unity, and a reminder that architecture is not just about building structures, but about building bridges between hearts and cultures.

As you stand on the Victoria Falls Bridge, with the awe-inspiring falls before you, remember that it's more than just a bridge; it's an embodiment of human potential, an emblem of cross-border camaraderie, and a testament to the idea that when nature and creativity intertwine, the results are as breathtaking as the cascade of water below. Let its legacy inspire you to design not just for function, but for the celebration of unity, the fostering of connection, and the transformative power of architectural wonders in the grand tapestry of human achievement.

73

Stonehenge, UK

Close your eyes and journey back in time to a windswept plain in England, where colossal stones stand in a mysterious and ancient arrangement – this is Stonehenge, a celestial marvel and a testament to the human spirit's connection to the cosmos. Allow me to transport you to a place where the past whispers its enigmatic secrets, and the present marvels at the ingenuity of our ancestors.

Imagine massive stones, some reaching up to 30 feet in height, arranged in concentric circles and horseshoe patterns. These stones aren't just rocks; they're gateways to a world of ancient knowledge and cosmic understanding. Stonehenge isn't just a monument; it's a celestial observatory, a place where our forebearers gazed upon the heavens and sought answers to the mysteries of existence.

The design of Stonehenge isn't just an arrangement of stones; it's a manifestation of reverence for the sun, moon, and stars. The alignment of these stones with celestial events, such as solstices and equinoxes, demonstrates a profound connection between humanity and the universe. Stonehenge's colossal trilithons and bluestones are a testament to the ingenious ways in which our ancestors harnessed the power of geometry and engineering to interact with the cosmos.

Imagine standing within the stone circle, feeling the energy of generations past who gathered here to celebrate the changing seasons, mark significant moments in time, and connect with the rhythms of the universe. Stonehenge isn't just a landmark; it's a gateway to the past, a symbol of humanity's timeless curiosity, and a reminder that the cosmos has inspired wonder and contemplation across cultures and eras.

Yet, Stonehenge's significance transcends its historical roots. It isn't just an archaeological site; it's a symbol of human curiosity, a beacon of spiritual significance, and a tribute to the timeless pursuit of understanding. It stands as a testament to the resilience of the human spirit, the enduring appeal of cosmic mysteries, and the interconnectedness of all cultures in their quest to comprehend the universe.

Imagine visitors from around the world, standing before Stonehenge, touched by its ancient aura and captivated by its cosmic allure. Imagine their shared sense of wonder, reminding us that regardless of our backgrounds, the desire to explore the mysteries of the cosmos unites us all.

Dreamers and seekers of knowledge, let Stonehenge's ancient wisdom and cosmic connection inspire your own quests for understanding and exploration. Just as its stones were positioned to align with the heavens, so too can your ideas align with the cosmic rhythms of creativity and discovery. Stonehenge's story whispers that every effort to understand the universe, every inquiry into the nature of existence, can be a tribute to the human spirit's curiosity, a celebration of our shared cosmic journey, and a reminder that the cosmos continues to inspire wonder and awe.

As you stand before Stonehenge, beneath the vast sky and surrounded by ancient stones, remember that it's more than just a monument; it's a bridge between humanity and the cosmos, an embodiment of human ingenuity, and a symbol of the eternal dialogue between humans and the universe. Let its legacy inspire you to design not just for the present, but for the exploration of the unknown, the preservation of ancient wisdom, and the transformative power of blending architecture and cosmic inspiration in the grand tapestry of human achievement.

74

Wat Rong Khun (White Temple), Thailand

Imagine a temple that emerges from the realm of mythology, a structure so dazzlingly white that it seems to have been crafted by celestial beings themselves. Welcome to Wat Rong Khun, the White Temple, a masterpiece that blurs the boundaries between architecture and art, tradition and modernity. Join me on a journey to a place where spirituality and creativity dance together in harmonious elegance.

Picture a temple as pure as snow, adorned with intricate carvings, shimmering glass mosaics, and delicate sculptures that narrate tales of virtue, struggle, and enlightenment. Wat Rong Khun isn't just a temple; it's a visual poem, a canvas of artistic expression that invites visitors to explore the depths of their souls.

The design of Wat Rong Khun isn't just architecture; it's a blend of ancient wisdom and contemporary vision, a fusion of spiritual resonance and avant-garde imagination. Its all-white exterior symbolizes purity, while the intricate details mirror the complexities of the human journey. The bridge leading to the temple is like crossing from the realm of the ordinary to the realm of enlightenment, a journey towards self-discovery and understanding.

Imagine stepping inside the temple, feeling a sense of serenity envelop you as you stand amidst sculptures of reaching hands and glowing beings. Wat Rong Khun isn't just a structure; it's a sanctuary of the soul, a place where traditional Buddhist teachings are woven with modern symbolism, reminding us of the universality of human struggles and aspirations.

Yet, its significance goes beyond its spiritual roots. Wat Rong Khun isn't just a religious site; it's a testament to the power of art to inspire, provoke, and transcend. It stands as a reminder that creativity can breathe new life into ancient traditions, and that architecture can be a canvas for profound messages of hope, unity, and transformation.

Imagine visitors from around the world, standing before Wat Rong Khun, awed by its otherworldly beauty and captivated by its thought-provoking symbolism. Imagine their shared sense of wonder, reminding us that regardless of our backgrounds, the pursuit of meaning, beauty, and enlightenment is a common thread that binds humanity.

Dreamers and seekers of inspiration, let Wat Rong Khun's ethereal beauty and symbolic depth ignite your own quests for artistic expression and spiritual growth. Just as the temple's intricate carvings tell stories, so too can your designs tell stories of human experience, resilience, and growth. Wat Rong Khun's story whispers that every creation born from the heart, every effort to fuse tradition and innovation, can be a tribute to the human spirit's boundless creativity, a celebration of cultural heritage, and a reminder that architecture can be a conduit for spiritual exploration.

As you stand before Wat Rong Khun, surrounded by its shimmering beauty and the lush landscape of Thailand, remember that it's more than just a temple; it's a manifestation of artistic vision, a reflection of spiritual longing, and a symbol of the eternal dance between creativity and enlightenment. Let its legacy inspire you to design not just for aesthetics, but for the elevation of the soul, the preservation of cultural identity, and the transformative power of blending art and spirituality in the grand tapestry of human achievement.

75

Rialto Bridge, Italy

Imagine strolling through the enchanting waterways of Venice, where history dances with the present and where elegance meets practicality. As you explore this labyrinth of canals, you come across a structure that seems to suspend itself over the water, gracefully connecting two worlds. This is the Rialto Bridge, a captivating marvel that encapsulates the essence of Venice's soul and ingenuity.

Visualize a majestic bridge with a single graceful arch, rising proudly above the Grand Canal. It's not just a bridge; it's a lifeline that links bustling markets and quiet alleys, a testament to the enduring power of human connection and commerce. The Rialto Bridge isn't merely an architectural feat; it's a testament to the Venetian spirit, where artistry and functionality harmonize seamlessly.

The design of the Rialto Bridge isn't just architecture; it's a celebration of engineering brilliance, an ode to the human capacity for creativity, and an embodiment of the Venetian reverence for beauty. Its elegant arch stands as a symbol of triumph over challenges, reflecting the city's resilience in the face of adversity, and its steps and shops evoke a sense of unity and shared experience that transcends time.

Imagine walking across the Rialto Bridge, feeling the centuries beneath your feet, and marveling at the bustling marketplace that has flourished here for generations. The Rialto Bridge isn't just a structure; it's a stage where history and everyday life coalesce, a testament to the importance of trade and culture in shaping the identity of a city.

Yet, its significance reaches beyond its utilitarian role. The Rialto Bridge isn't just a passage; it's a symbol of Venice's cultural heritage, a testament to the city's artistic legacy, and a bridge between past and present. It stands as a reminder that architecture is more than bricks and mortar; it's a vessel that carries the stories and dreams of a city's inhabitants, and an embodiment of their aspirations.

Imagine travelers from across the globe, standing before the Rialto Bridge, captivated by its timeless beauty and historical significance. Their shared sense of wonder reminds us that despite our diverse origins, the pursuit of connection, culture, and shared experiences unites humanity.

Dreamers and admirers of beauty, let the Rialto Bridge's timeless charm and functional elegance inspire your own quests for creative solutions and enduring impact. Just as the bridge unites two banks, so too can your designs unite functionality and aesthetics, history and innovation. The Rialto Bridge's story whispers that every creation born from necessity and beauty, every effort to blend tradition and modernity, can be a tribute to human ingenuity, a celebration of cultural heritage, and a reminder that architecture can be a testament to the unbreakable bonds that connect us all.

As you stand before the Rialto Bridge, amidst the vibrant energy of Venice and the serenity of its canals, remember that it's more than just a bridge; it's a living monument to human interaction, a reflection of Venetian identity, and a symbol of the enduring power of bridges, both physical and metaphorical, to connect us to the past, the present, and each other. Let its legacy inspire you to design not just for aesthetics, but for the enrichment of human experiences, the preservation of cultural narratives, and the transformative power of blending history and innovation in the grand tapestry of human achievement.

76

Edinburgh Castle, UK

Imagine standing atop an ancient volcanic rock, gazing out over the charming city of Edinburgh, Scotland. There, perched majestically against the sky, is Edinburgh Castle, a remarkable testament to human history, ingenuity, and the enduring spirit of a nation.

Picture a castle that seems to rise directly from the rugged terrain, as if it's an extension of the very earth it stands upon. This is Edinburgh Castle, a place where history and myth intertwine, where time stands still amidst the bustling city below. Its stone walls tell stories that echo through centuries, capturing the essence of Scotland's past, present, and future.

Edinburgh Castle isn't just a fortress; it's a living memory of battles fought and won, of kings and queens who held court within its walls, and of the people who call Scotland home. It's a guardian of legends, a sentinel of tradition, and a repository of treasures that unfold the pages of Scotland's complex narrative.

The castle's design isn't just about walls and turrets; it's a reflection of a nation's resilience and creativity. Perched on Castle Rock, it is a physical embodiment of the Scottish spirit, fortified against adversity and reaching towards the heavens. Its strategic placement speaks of a time when protection was paramount, and its grandeur pays homage to the people who built it.

Walking through the castle's gateways, you are stepping into a realm where the past feels vividly present. The ancient stone halls, regal chambers, and military structures remind us that architecture is more than bricks; it's a vessel for memories, a canvas for history, and a space where human stories are etched into the very fabric of the walls.

As you stand within the walls of Edinburgh Castle, it's hard not to feel the weight of centuries, the echoes of the past mingling with the vitality of the present. This castle isn't just a relic; it's a bridge that spans generations, connecting us to the struggles and triumphs of those who came before us.

In its towering presence, Edinburgh Castle carries a reminder that the strength of a nation isn't just found in its armies, but in its cultural heritage and the unity of its people. It has been a witness to the evolution of Scotland, a sentinel guarding its treasures, and a source of inspiration for those who seek to understand the past while shaping the future.

Let Edinburgh Castle's enduring presence inspire you to build not just structures, but legacies that withstand the test of time. Just as its walls have preserved the stories of a nation, your designs can be vessels that capture the spirit of your own times and leave a mark on the landscape of history. Just as the castle's silhouette against the Scottish sky inspires awe, let your work inspire others to reach for the heights of creativity and impact, forging connections between the past, the present, and the dreams of tomorrow.

77

Space Needle, USA

Imagine standing on the cusp of innovation, your gaze lifted towards the heavens, and there it stands: the Space Needle, an iconic emblem of human imagination, aspiration, and the unending quest to reach for the stars.

Rising proudly against the Seattle skyline like a futuristic beacon, the Space

Needle isn't just a structure; it's a testament to human ingenuity and the boundless possibilities that lie beyond our earthly confines. It's as if a sci-fi novel has come to life, inviting us to join in an adventure of discovery and exploration.

Picture the Space Needle's sleek, tapering form, inspired by the elegant lines of a spaceship. It's not merely a building; it's a gateway to the future, a symbol of the human spirit's desire to break free from the constraints of the familiar and explore the unknown. Its design whispers of sleek rockets and interstellar travel, inviting us to ponder the mysteries of the universe.

But the Space Needle isn't just about looks; it's about pushing the boundaries of what's possible. When it was built for the 1962 World's Fair, it was a feat of engineering brilliance, showcasing the audacious spirit of a generation that dared to dream big. Its rotating observation deck offers a panoramic view of the city below, reminding us that when we strive for greatness, we gain new perspectives that can change our world.

Standing beneath the Space Needle's graceful spire, one can't help but feel a sense of connection to all those who came before, those visionaries who dared to look up and dream. It's a reminder that history is built by those who reach for the stars, and that the ripples of their aspirations continue to inspire us to this day.

The Space Needle isn't just a tribute to the past; it's a symbol of the future we're still building. Its towering presence beckons us to keep asking questions, to keep challenging the limits of our knowledge, and to keep searching for answers among the stars. It's a call to dream boldly and embrace the unknown, just as those who first conceived of the Space Needle did decades ago.

As you stand in the shadow of the Space Needle, let it remind you that the sky is not the limit; it's only the beginning. Just as this iconic structure reaches for the cosmos, your own endeavors can stretch beyond the boundaries of what's been done before. Let it inspire you to innovate, to design, and to create in ways that change the world, reminding us all that the universe is vast and full of possibilities waiting to be explored.

78

Museum of the Future, UAE

Close your eyes and envision a structure that seems to have emerged from the pages of a science fiction novel, a marvel that embraces the future with open arms. This is the Museum of the Future, a remarkable fusion of imagination and innovation nestled in the heart of Dubai, United Arab Emirates.

Imagine a building that defies convention, a structure that bends and twists, almost as if it's shaping its own destiny. The Museum of the Future isn't just a place to house relics; it's a living testament to the boundless possibilities of human creativity and progress. Its design challenges our perception of what architecture can be, a blend of artistry and technology that invites us to explore what lies ahead.

As you approach the museum, you're met with a mesmerizing façade adorned with intricate patterns, like a shimmering code that holds the secrets of tomorrow. It's not just a building; it's a symbol of our endless quest for knowledge, the embodiment of the belief that through innovation, we can shape a better world.

Built in the heart of Dubai's innovation district, the Museum of the Future is a nod to the UAE's dedication to pushing the boundaries of what's possible. It's not just a place to preserve the past; it's a beacon guiding us towards the future. Inside its walls, you'll find a space where science, technology, and art intertwine, a playground for dreamers and thinkers alike.

But the Museum of the Future isn't just a testament to advanced architecture; it's a reminder that our journey as a species is a story of evolution, of constant growth and adaptation. It's a place where ideas come to life, where the seeds of innovation are sown, and where the future is being forged in real time.

Standing before this architectural wonder, let it inspire you to embrace change, to think beyond the confines of today, and to question the limits of tomorrow. Let it remind you that the future isn't a distant destination; it's a canvas waiting for the strokes of our creativity. Just as the Museum of the Future challenges tradition, let your own ideas break free from convention and embrace the infinite possibilities that lie ahead.

In the shadow of this captivating building, remember that you too have the power to shape the future. Just as the Museum of the Future stands as a testament to the power of human ingenuity, let your innovations be the building blocks of a world yet to be imagined—a world where dreams and reality intertwine, creating a legacy that future generations will look upon with wonder and admiration.

79

Borobudur, Indonesia

Imagine a colossal puzzle of stone rising from the lush landscapes of Indonesia, a testament to the human spirit's journey towards enlightenment and transcendence. This is Borobudur, an awe-inspiring temple that reaches towards the heavens while grounding us in the beauty of our earthly existence.

Picture yourself wandering through a complex labyrinth of intricately carved panels, each one telling a story, inviting you to unravel the mysteries of a distant past. Borobudur isn't just a building; it's a living encyclopedia of human history and spirituality, a testament to our yearning for wisdom and understanding.

Built in the 9th century on the island of Java, Borobudur is a masterpiece of design that merges art, architecture, and philosophy. Its unique structure consists of several tiers, symbolizing the stages of enlightenment according to Buddhist teachings. As you ascend its terraces, you're metaphorically ascending the path to enlightenment, leaving behind the mundane concerns of the world below.

The intricate carvings that adorn its walls are like whispers from the past, stories of devotion, myths, and lessons that have been passed down through generations. They tell tales of compassion, perseverance, and the intricate interplay between humanity and the universe.

As the sun rises over Borobudur, it bathes the temple in a warm, golden glow, casting shadows that seem to dance along the ancient stones. This daily ritual reminds us that just as the sun brings light to darkness, Borobudur symbolizes a path out of ignorance and towards the light of wisdom.

Borobudur's influence isn't limited to the realm of architecture; it's a testament to the enduring power of human creativity, belief, and the quest for meaning. It's a reminder that across time and cultures, we share a common longing to understand our place in the cosmos.

Standing in the shadow of Borobudur, you're surrounded by a profound sense of interconnectedness, a reminder that we're all on a journey towards greater awareness and enlightenment. Let it inspire you to embrace the pursuit of knowledge, to seek answers to life's mysteries, and to appreciate the intricate beauty of the world around you.

In the presence of this extraordinary structure, remember that just as Borobudur has stood the test of time, so can your own contributions to the world. Let your endeavors be a reflection of your inner quest for growth and understanding, a reminder that our shared journey towards enlightenment is one that transcends cultures, generations, and time itself.

80

Gardens by the Bay, Singapore

Close your eyes and imagine a realm where nature and technology dance together in perfect harmony, a utopian oasis nestled in the heart of a bustling city. This is Gardens by the Bay, a breathtaking fusion of innovation and nature's splendor that transports you to a world where dreams and reality intertwine.

Envision towering trees that seem to touch the sky, their branches adorned with vibrant blooms that defy gravity. These are the iconic Supertrees of Gardens by the Bay, a testament to human creativity and a reminder of the beauty and importance of our natural world. But these trees are not just aesthetic wonders; they're marvels of technology, housing a network of solar cells that power the garden's nightly light show.

Set against the backdrop of Singapore's futuristic skyline, Gardens by the Bay is a testament to the city-state's commitment to sustainability and environmental consciousness. It's a sanctuary where visitors can escape the urban hustle and immerse themselves in the soothing embrace of nature.

The centerpiece of this enchanting garden is the Cloud Forest Dome—a lush, mist-covered haven that houses a stunning indoor waterfall. As you walk through this ecosystem, you're transported to a realm of serenity, where the air is cool and the sights and sounds of a tropical rainforest envelop you.

But Gardens by the Bay isn't just a place of beauty; it's a symbol of humanity's responsibility to protect and nurture the planet we call home. It's a beacon that encourages us to embrace sustainable practices, to seek harmony between urban development and the natural world, and to strive for a future where technology and nature coexist in harmony.

As you stroll through the pathways, let the beauty of Gardens by the Bay inspire you to become a steward of the earth, to appreciate the intricate balance of ecosystems, and to take steps towards a more sustainable future. Let it remind you that innovation and nature need not be adversaries, but partners in creating a world that's not only prosperous but also nurturing to all forms of life.

In the presence of these wondrous gardens, remember that just as the Supertrees rise towards the sky, so too can your own aspirations and dreams. Let Gardens by the Bay be a testament to the power of human creativity and the remarkable resilience of nature, encouraging you to seek balance and harmony in all aspects of life, and to leave a legacy that resonates with the beauty and wonder of this remarkable place.

81

The Milan Cathedral (Duomo di Milano), Italy

Imagine standing in the heart of Milan, Italy, gazing up at a masterpiece that seems to touch the very sky itself – The Milan Cathedral, or Duomo di Milano. This awe-inspiring architectural gem is not merely a cathedral; it's a symphony of creativity, faith, and innovation that has been echoing through the annals of time.

Rising from the vibrant cityscape, the Duomo di Milano is a true testament to human dedication and artistic vision. Its construction began in the 14th century and continued for centuries, a labor of love that spanned generations. The cathedral's intricate facade is adorned with a mesmerizing array of sculptures, intricate carvings, and ornate details that narrate biblical stories and historical events.

The cathedral's unique and philosophical design embodies the essence of the Italian Renaissance – a period that celebrated the harmonious blend of art, science, and spirituality. Its innovative architecture, characterized by its Gothic style, features an impressive network of soaring spires and intricate flying buttresses that seem to defy the limits of gravity. The interior is equally enchanting, with grand arches, stunning stained glass windows, and a sense of divine space that embraces anyone who enters.

Beyond its stunning aesthetics, the Milan Cathedral holds deep historical and cultural significance. It's not just a religious site, but a living chronicle of Milan's evolution and resilience through the ages. From hosting imperial ceremonies to witnessing historical events, this magnificent edifice has stood witness to the ebb and flow of history. Its influence is immeasurable, as it continues to inspire awe and admiration in all who visit, reminding us of the extraordinary capabilities of human creativity, determination, and devotion.

Visiting the Milan Cathedral is like stepping into a portal that bridges the past and the present, inviting us to reflect on the timeless pursuit of beauty, faith, and architectural brilliance. It stands not only as a tribute to the craftsmanship of its creators but as a beacon of inspiration for generations to come – a reminder that the heights of human achievement are limited only by the boundaries of our imagination and determination.

82

The Chrysler Building, USA

Picture the New York City skyline, a realm of towering skyscrapers that reach for the heavens. Among these architectural giants, the Chrysler Building stands as a beacon of innovation, elegance, and a testament to the human spirit's pursuit of greatness.

The Chrysler Building, nestled in the heart of Manhattan, is a symbol of the roaring 1920s – an era of boundless ambition and artistic fervor. Its background is woven with the aspirations of its time, a race for supremacy in the race for the world's tallest building. Designed by the visionary architect William Van Alen, its construction was an exercise in both architectural ingenuity and fierce competition.

What sets the Chrysler Building apart is its unique and philosophical design, blending Art Deco elements with a distinct automotive influence. The gleaming stainless steel spire, adorned with intricate ornamentation, stretches upwards towards the sky, invoking a sense of motion and progress. This melding of art and industry reflects the spirit of the age, a celebration of modernity and aspiration.

The Chrysler Building's innovative architecture is nothing short of breathtaking. The artistry lies not only in its exterior grandeur but also in the details that define its interior – from the stunning lobby adorned with luxurious materials to the Art Deco-inspired elevator doors. Its influence on architectural history is immense; it marked a new era of skyscraper design and spurred competition for architectural supremacy, shaping the skyline of New York City and beyond.

In the tapestry of history, the Chrysler Building is a testament to the boundless potential of human creativity and determination. It serves as a reminder that even in the face of challenges, innovation and beauty can thrive. As you gaze upon its majestic form, you're not just witnessing an iconic building; you're connecting with a legacy of ambition, design excellence, and the everlasting pursuit of reaching new heights – both architecturally and metaphorically.

83

National Monument, Indonesia

Imagine standing before a colossal masterpiece that embodies a nation's struggle, resilience, and unity – the National Monument of Indonesia, also known as Monas. It stands proudly in the heart of Jakarta, an iconic landmark that tells a story of a nation's journey towards independence and its unwavering spirit.

The National Monument holds a profound background, rooted in Indonesia's history. This towering structure was unveiled in 1975 to commemorate the nation's hard-fought independence from colonial rule. Designed by the celebrated Indonesian architect Frederich Silaban, its form draws inspiration from ancient Indonesian architecture, melding traditional motifs with modern symbolism.

At first glance, the National Monument's unique and philosophical design is awe-inspiring. Rising 132 meters into the sky, the monument's gleaming white obelisk reaches upward, symbolizing the aspirations of a nation reaching for progress and unity. Its base features a meticulously designed relief that chronicles Indonesia's historical journey, while a gold-leaf flame crowns the structure, representing the nation's eternal spirit.

The innovative architecture of the National Monument reflects not just the physical but also the emotional journey of Indonesia. Beyond its visual grandeur, the monument carries immense cultural and historical significance. It's a symbol of hope, resilience, and the sacrifices made by countless individuals to forge a free and united Indonesia. The monument's influence on history is immeasurable – it's a focal point of national pride and a gathering place for celebrations, ceremonies, and reflections on the nation's past and future.

As you stand before the National Monument, you're not just witnessing a remarkable architectural marvel; you're connecting with the soul of a nation. The monument's presence resonates with the indomitable human spirit, reminding us that in the face of challenges, unity and determination can shape a brighter future. It's a living testament to the power of collective dreams, and its story invites us all to embrace our own journeys with courage and conviction.

84

Kota Tua, Indonesia

Transport yourself back in time to the enchanting heart of Jakarta, where history comes alive in every cobblestone and weathered façade of Kota Tua, also known as Old Batavia. Nestled amidst the bustling metropolis, this iconic area is a treasure trove of stories, capturing the essence of Indonesia's colonial past and cultural evolution.

Kota Tua's background is a tapestry woven with the threads of centuries. Once a vibrant hub of the Dutch East India Company, the area's history dates back to the 17th century when it was established as the center of trade and commerce. The architecture reflects a charming blend of Dutch colonial, Chinese, and indigenous Indonesian influences, each brick and building whispering tales of the diverse cultures that converged here.

Walking through Kota Tua is like stepping into a living museum, where every street corner holds a unique piece of history. The unique and philosophical design of the area lies in its preservation of the past amidst a rapidly changing present. Cobblestone streets wind past stately buildings adorned with intricate carvings, while open squares invite locals and visitors to gather, creating an ambiance that's both nostalgic and contemporary.

Kota Tua's innovative architecture is a testament to its enduring relevance. The area serves as a bridge between eras, allowing us to glimpse the lives of those who walked these streets centuries ago. As the birthplace of Jakarta, it holds an unmatched influence on the city's cultural identity. More than just a historic site, Kota Tua is a vibrant canvas where art, heritage, and modern life converge. It hosts markets, festivals, and cultural events that celebrate Indonesia's rich heritage, fostering a sense of pride and belonging among its people.

In the heart of Kota Tua, you're not merely a spectator of history – you're an active participant in its ongoing narrative. The area's charm lies not only in its architectural beauty but in its ability to connect the past and the present, reminding us that our stories are intricately linked with those who came before us. As you explore the winding streets and gaze upon the majestic buildings, you're invited to ponder the threads that connect us to our roots and inspire us to shape the future while honoring our past.

85

Bellagio Hotel & Casino, USA

Nestled like a gem in the heart of the bustling Las Vegas Strip, the Bellagio Hotel & Casino stands as a true testament to the grandeur and extravagance that defines the spirit of Las Vegas. It's not just a hotel – it's a destination that transports visitors into a world of luxury, entertainment, and architectural marvel.

The Bellagio's background is a tale of vision and ambition. Inspired by the picturesque village of Bellagio on Lake Como in Italy, its creators set out to bring a touch of European elegance to the desert city of Las Vegas. Since its opening in 1998, the Bellagio has become an iconic landmark, setting the bar for luxury hospitality and entertainment in the city that never sleeps.

What truly sets the Bellagio apart is its unique and philosophical design, which marries opulence with artistry. The pièce de résistance is the iconic dancing fountains that choreograph water, light, and music into a mesmerizing symphony. The elegant Conservatory and Botanical Gardens inside the hotel are transformed seasonally into breathtaking floral displays that evoke wonder and awe. This harmonious fusion of nature, art, and luxury reflects the ethos of the Bellagio – a space that seeks to provide an oasis of indulgence and inspiration.

The Bellagio's innovative architecture and influence go beyond its exterior façade. Its commitment to excellence has set a benchmark for the hospitality industry, raising the bar for accommodations, dining, and entertainment. From world-class restaurants helmed by renowned chefs to its legendary casino and captivating performances, the Bellagio has redefined the Las Vegas experience. It's not just a hotel and casino; it's a place where dreams are pursued, memories are made, and the ordinary is transformed into the extraordinary.

As you stand in awe of the Bellagio's iconic fountains, surrounded by the glitz and glamour of the Las Vegas Strip, you're reminded that life is meant to be lived to the fullest. It's a symbol of the human spirit's ability to create something magical out of the ordinary, to craft experiences that delight the senses and stir the soul. The Bellagio is more than a building; it's an embodiment of the pursuit of pleasure, the celebration of life, and the power of imagination to turn dreams into reality.

86

Hudson Yards, USA

Nestled on the vibrant island of Manhattan, Hudson Yards emerges as a modern marvel that perfectly encapsulates the dynamic spirit of New York City. More than just a collection of buildings, Hudson Yards is a testament to innovation, urban transformation, and the boundless human imagination.

Hudson Yards was born out of a vision to create a new neighborhood in the heart of the city – a place where sleek skyscrapers, lush parks, and cultural venues harmoniously coexist. Its background is rooted in the relentless pursuit of progress, reflecting New York's perpetual desire to reinvent itself. Opening its doors in 2019, Hudson Yards was designed to redefine urban living and offer a glimpse into the future of sustainable, interconnected communities.

The unique and philosophical design of Hudson Yards is a masterpiece of contemporary urban planning. The crown jewel of the development, the Vessel, stands as an intricate honeycomb-like structure that invites visitors to explore its spiral staircases and platforms while offering breathtaking views of the city. This embodies the essence of Hudson Yards – a place that fosters connectivity, exploration, and human interaction.

Innovative architecture defines Hudson Yards as a world of its own. The soaring skyscrapers feature cutting-edge design and eco-friendly elements, setting new standards for sustainability in urban development. The High Line, an elevated park built on repurposed railway tracks, seamlessly weaves through the district, offering a serene escape from the urban hustle.

Hudson Yards' influence on history is profound, signaling a transformative chapter in the city's narrative. It showcases the power of human ingenuity to reshape urban landscapes, reimagine communal spaces, and embrace sustainable living. The development's cultural venues, public art installations, and diverse experiences reflect the cosmopolitan essence of New York, celebrating the city's rich diversity and pioneering spirit.

As you walk through Hudson Yards, you're reminded that the city is a living canvas, where creativity knows no bounds. It's a testament to our ability to construct not just buildings, but vibrant communities that capture the essence of a city's soul. Hudson Yards encourages us to dream big, push boundaries, and shape the urban spaces of tomorrow, while honoring the traditions that make each city truly unique.

87

Rockefeller Center, USA

Nestled amidst the bustling heart of Manhattan, the Rockefeller Center stands as a timeless emblem of human aspiration and creativity. This iconic complex, spanning 22 acres, isn't just a collection of buildings; it's a testament to the indomitable spirit of innovation, and a tribute to the power of human collaboration.

Conceived during the Great Depression, the Rockefeller Center was a visionary response to the need for urban rejuvenation and communal spaces that inspire. Emerging during the early 20th century, this remarkable hub has transformed over the years into a symbol of resilience and progress.

The design of the Rockefeller Center embodies a unique blend of architectural magnificence and philosophical intent. The Art Deco style that adorns its buildings exudes an elegance that transcends eras, paying homage to the optimism of the time. The centerpiece, the iconic Prometheus statue, symbolizes enlightenment and human potential, reflecting the belief that art and knowledge can illuminate even the darkest times.

Innovative architecture defines the Rockefeller Center, not just in its buildings but also in the very way it shapes communal spaces. The ice-skating rink that transforms into a sparkling wonderland during the holidays, and the mesmerizing Radio City Music Hall, showcase a harmonious blend of artistic expression and urban functionality. The underground concourses and rooftop gardens illustrate a thoughtful approach to urban planning, maximizing the usage of space for both work and leisure.

The Rockefeller Center's influence on history transcends its physical presence. Its annual Christmas Tree Lighting ceremony has become a global symbol of hope and unity, a reminder that even in challenging times, the human spirit can shine bright. Moreover, the complex's pivotal role in New York's cultural scene, from hosting art exhibitions to live performances, speaks to its enduring relevance and impact.

Walking through the Rockefeller Center, you're immersed in a microcosm of human achievement. It urges us to believe in the power of dreams, to recognize that innovation thrives in the face of adversity, and that creativity can shape both our surroundings and our collective spirit. It's a place where history and modernity dance hand in hand, inviting us to be a part of a legacy that continues to inspire generations.

88

9/11 Memorial & Museum, USA

In the heart of Lower Manhattan, the 9/11 Memorial & Museum stands as a solemn tribute to the resilience of the human spirit and a testament to the power of unity in the face of tragedy. This iconic site, situated at the former

World Trade Center, honors the memory of those who lost their lives during the devastating events of September 11, 2001.

Born from the collective resolve to never forget, the 9/11 Memorial & Museum emerged as a profound way to honor the lives lost and to acknowledge the shared pain of a nation. The twin reflecting pools, set within the footprints of the original Twin Towers, cascade with serene beauty, while the Survivor Tree symbolizes strength and renewal. The museum's underground galleries, designed with a deep sense of reverence, house artifacts and narratives that bear witness to the resilience of individuals and communities.

The design and architecture of the 9/11 Memorial & Museum are both striking and deeply thoughtful. The architects aimed not just to create a space of remembrance, but also a space of healing and contemplation. The vastness of the reflecting pools, the solemnity of the inscribed names, and the intimate stories within the museum itself evoke a sense of interconnectedness that transcends time and boundaries.

Influential beyond its physical presence, the 9/11 Memorial & Museum serves as a touchstone for collective memory and unity. It reminds us that amid darkness, there is light; in the face of unimaginable pain, there is resilience. The memorial's impact extends to its role in fostering dialogue, understanding, and compassion, inviting us to reflect on the broader implications of the events that unfolded on that fateful day.

Visiting the 9/11 Memorial & Museum is a journey of remembrance, contemplation, and hope. It implores us to honor the past while looking towards the future with renewed empathy and determination. This iconic site stands not only as a tribute to history, but also as a testament to the boundless strength of the human spirit to rise above adversity, rebuild, and stand united.

89

One Vanderbilt, USA

100 ICONIC BUILDINGS WITH UNIQUE DESIGN AND ARCHITECTURE

Rising majestically amidst the iconic New York City skyline, One Vanderbilt stands as a testament to innovation, progress, and the enduring spirit of ambition. This remarkable skyscraper, located near Grand Central Terminal, is not only a symbol of architectural prowess but also a shining example of urban renewal and connectivity.

One Vanderbilt's journey began with a vision to transform Midtown Manhattan into a modern, sustainable urban oasis. This towering masterpiece was designed to seamlessly blend into the city's historic fabric while redefining its skyline. The building's distinctive form, characterized by its sleek, tapering silhouette, draws inspiration from New York's iconic Art Deco architecture, paying homage to the city's rich heritage.

What truly sets One Vanderbilt apart is its commitment to both form and function. Its design prioritizes sustainability, energy efficiency, and human experience. The expansive public spaces and retail areas at its base invite bustling urban life, while the vertical gardens and open-air observation deck offer a respite from the fast-paced city. The crown jewel of its design, however, is the Grand Central Terminal's direct connection, a testament to its role in fostering connectivity and enhancing the city's infrastructure.

In the annals of history, One Vanderbilt's influence is profound. It symbolizes New York's unyielding spirit of progress and its ability to adapt while respecting its heritage. Beyond its architectural marvel, the skyscraper stands as a beacon of inspiration for cities worldwide, urging them to embrace innovation, sustainability, and community-centered design. One Vanderbilt, with its towering presence and profound purpose, invites us to gaze upwards not just at its heights, but at the limitless possibilities that urban design can bring to life.

90

TCL Chinese Theatre, USA

Amid the glittering lights of Hollywood, the TCL Chinese Theatre stands as a symbol of glamour, entertainment, and the magic of the silver screen. This legendary movie palace is more than just a theater; it's a historical monument that has witnessed the dreams of stars and the awe of millions who have walked its hallowed halls.

The story of the TCL Chinese Theatre began in the heart of Hollywood's golden era. Opening its doors in 1927, it quickly became the epicenter of movie premieres, attracting the biggest names in the film industry. Its ornate Chinese-inspired architecture, adorned with intricate dragons, pagodas, and stone lions, lent an air of mystique and grandeur to the cinema experience.

What makes the TCL Chinese Theatre truly iconic is its famed forecourt, paved with over 200 handprints, footprints, and signatures of Hollywood's most revered stars. As you walk across these imprints, you're treading in the footsteps of legends, connecting with their legacies in a tangible way. The theater's design and architectural motifs remind us that the world of cinema is not just about watching movies, but about immersing ourselves in stories that capture our hearts and minds.

Throughout history, the TCL Chinese Theatre has played a pivotal role in shaping the entertainment industry. From hosting glamorous movie premieres to being a cultural touchstone during significant events, it has held a mirror to the evolution of cinema and celebrity culture. Its enduring influence is a testament to the enduring power of storytelling and the impact of the silver screen on our lives, reminding us that within its walls, dreams are realized and legends are born.

91

Griffith Observatory, USA

Perched atop the scenic hills of Los Angeles, the Griffith Observatory is a beacon of knowledge, wonder, and discovery. This iconic building has served as a gateway to the cosmos for generations, inviting both stargazers and curious minds to explore the mysteries of the universe.

Built in the 1930s, the Griffith Observatory was envisioned as a place where the public could freely access the wonders of astronomy. Its distinctive Art Deco design, with gleaming white columns and domes, reflects a blend of architectural elegance and a passion for celestial exploration. The observatory's strategic location allows visitors to marvel at panoramic views of the sprawling city below while also offering a clear glimpse into the boundless expanse of the night sky.

But the Griffith Observatory is more than just a building; it's a sanctuary for cosmic contemplation. Its planetarium and exhibits transport visitors on a journey through space and time, helping them grasp the vastness of our universe and the interconnectedness of all things. The observatory's philosophical design encourages us to ponder our place in the cosmos and our quest for understanding the mysteries beyond our world.

Over the years, the Griffith Observatory has served as a place of both education and inspiration. It has been featured in numerous films, making it a familiar landmark to people around the world. Its impact extends beyond its architectural beauty, as it has fueled countless imaginations and ignited a passion for science and astronomy in generations of visitors. Standing beneath its iconic dome, we are reminded of the human spirit's innate desire to explore, learn, and reach for the stars.

92

Tokyo Tower, Japan

Rising gracefully from the heart of Tokyo's vibrant skyline, Tokyo Tower stands as a testament to Japan's modernity and its reverence for tradition. This iconic structure, resembling a radiant blend of Western influence and Japanese artistry, serves not only as a communication hub but also as a symbol of unity, innovation, and cultural identity.

Erected in 1958, Tokyo Tower was envisioned as a beacon of progress and hope, a tangible representation of Japan's post-war resurgence. Its graceful lattice design, inspired by the Eiffel Tower, showcases the nation's ability to blend Western architectural concepts with its own distinct sensibilities. The tower's vibrant orange hue, a color scientifically chosen to stand out amidst Tokyo's urban landscape, exudes a sense of warmth and optimism that resonates with both locals and visitors.

Beyond its physical form, Tokyo Tower's philosophical design encourages us to reflect on the harmonious coexistence of tradition and modernity. Its observatories offer breathtaking views of Tokyo's juxtaposition of ancient temples and bustling metropolis, reminding us of the delicate balance between honoring heritage and embracing progress. As a communication and broadcasting hub, Tokyo Tower has played a pivotal role in connecting people, fostering a sense of community, and disseminating knowledge to the masses.

Throughout its history, Tokyo Tower has maintained its relevance as a symbol of Japan's resilience, adaptability, and boundless aspirations. It has witnessed the nation's growth, evolution, and cultural shifts, serving as a silent witness to the dreams and aspirations of millions. Just as it illuminates Tokyo's night sky, Tokyo Tower illuminates the path forward, inspiring us to bridge the gap between tradition and innovation and to reach new heights in our own journeys.

93

Macau Tower Convention and Entertainment Center, China

MACAU TOWER CONVENTION AND ENTERTAINMENT CENTER, CHINA

Amid the bustling cityscape of Macau, the Macau Tower Convention and Entertainment Center stands as a beacon of modernity and cultural richness. This iconic structure, a fusion of architectural brilliance and artistic inspiration, not only graces the skyline but also symbolizes Macau's journey of transformation and harmony between tradition and progress.

Completed in the year 2001, the Macau Tower was conceived to encapsulate the essence of Macau's dynamic identity—a city that embraces its past while embracing the future. Its sleek and contemporary design, coupled with its intricate lattice structure, pays homage to the city's Portuguese heritage and its modern aspirations. The tower's towering height, at over 1,100 feet, is not just a physical achievement but a reflection of Macau's ambitions to reach new horizons.

The unique design of the Macau Tower is more than just an architectural feat; it carries a philosophical message of unity. Its structure is a testament to the harmony between man and nature, a principle deeply rooted in Chinese philosophy. The tower's strategic positioning on the waterfront allows it to blend seamlessly with the surrounding environment, inviting contemplation on the coexistence of urban development and the preservation of natural beauty.

In the rich tapestry of Macau's history, the Macau Tower holds a special place. It has witnessed the city's evolution from a colonial outpost to a thriving global destination for entertainment, culture, and business. As a hub for conventions, events, and adventure activities, the tower has catalyzed Macau's economic growth and positioned it on the global stage. It stands as a testament to Macau's ability to balance heritage and innovation, tradition and progress, and serves as an inspiration for all of us to embark on our own journeys of transformation, where the past and the future coalesce in perfect harmony.

94

Dubai Frame, UAE

DUBAI FRAME, UAE

Rising like a majestic gateway between Dubai's glittering past and its soaring future, the Dubai Frame stands as a testament to the city's audacious vision and boundless creativity. This iconic architectural marvel, conceived as a symbol of embracing heritage and innovation, encapsulates the heart and soul of Dubai's remarkable journey from humble beginnings to a global metropolis.

Completed in 2018, the Dubai Frame is not merely a building but a bridge through time, a harmonious marriage of past and present. Its awe-inspiring design resembles a colossal picture frame, elegantly framing the contrasting landscapes of Old Dubai and the modern skyline. This deliberate juxtaposition of architectural styles speaks to Dubai's embrace of its cultural roots while ceaselessly reaching for the sky.

The unique design of the Dubai Frame isn't just a matter of aesthetics—it carries a philosophical message. As visitors ascend through the frame's transparent elevator, they transition from the past to the future, metaphorically stepping into a journey of progress. The frame's reflective surfaces compel introspection, encouraging us to contemplate the passage of time and our role in shaping the future.

In the chronicles of Dubai's history, the Dubai Frame represents a pivotal chapter. It serves as a visual reminder of the city's remarkable transformation from a humble fishing village to a global hub of innovation and luxury. Its towering presence isn't just about height; it symbolizes the city's soaring aspirations, a testament to what can be achieved with audacity, ambition, and dedication.

The Dubai Frame isn't just a structure; it's an embodiment of human potential and the power of vision. It echoes Dubai's unwavering spirit of pushing boundaries, a call to all to dream big and turn those dreams into reality. As you stand before the frame, you can't help but be inspired to look beyond limitations, embrace the past, and pave the way for a future that's as grand as the Dubai Frame itself.

95

Transamerica Pyramid, USA

Behold the Transamerica Pyramid, a resplendent testament to human ingenuity rising proudly against the San Francisco skyline. This iconic skyscraper isn't just a building; it's a beacon of aspiration and innovation, a true architectural gem that embodies the spirit of progress and limitless possibilities.

Completed in 1972, the Transamerica Pyramid stands as a symbol of San Francisco's resilience and forward-thinking ethos. Its distinctive pyramid shape, a soaring 853 feet tall, captures the imagination with its sleek lines and audacious design. More than just a towering structure, it's a representation of reaching for the stars while staying grounded in history.

The pyramid's unique design isn't just an artistic choice; it reflects a philosophical connection to ancient symbols of strength and stability. Its tapered shape optimizes the use of space and sunlight, while the setbacks and terraces offer panoramic views of the city and the Bay beyond. This harmony between form and function encapsulates the idea of balance between nature and progress.

As one gazes upon the Transamerica Pyramid, it's impossible not to be transported back in time to San Francisco's dynamic history. It emerged during an era of architectural innovation, exemplifying the city's resilience after earthquakes and fires. Beyond its physical presence, the pyramid represents San Francisco's enduring spirit, constantly pushing boundaries to overcome challenges and reinvent itself.

The Transamerica Pyramid continues to play a significant role in San Francisco's identity. It's more than a landmark; it's a reminder that dreams can be realized through a blend of vision, hard work, and boldness. Its influence isn't confined to its impressive silhouette; it echoes the idea that every challenge is an opportunity to create something extraordinary, to rise above adversity and shine brightly, just like the apex of the Transamerica Pyramid against the California sky.

96

Coit Tower, USA

Welcome to Coit Tower, a majestic sentinel that graces the heart of San Francisco's skyline with its undeniable charm and artistic allure. Nestled atop Telegraph Hill, this iconic structure isn't merely a tower; it's a testament to community spirit, artistic expression, and the power of creative inspiration.

Constructed in 1933 as a tribute to the city's firefighters, Coit Tower stands as a beacon of appreciation and gratitude. But it's more than just a memorial; it's a living canvas that hosts a breathtaking collection of murals depicting scenes of everyday life during the Great Depression. These murals, created by talented artists as part of the Public Works of Art Project, narrate stories of resilience, unity, and hope.

What sets Coit Tower apart is not just its historical significance, but its visionary design. Rising 210 feet, the tower's art deco architecture captures the essence of the era it was born in. Its sleek lines and commanding presence reflect the spirit of progress and optimism that defined the 1930s.

Yet, there's a deeper layer to Coit Tower's influence. It's a reminder that art and community have the power to heal and uplift, even in the darkest of times. The murals inside the tower tell stories of ordinary people, portraying their struggles and aspirations. They remind us that creativity and expression can bridge gaps and bring people together, fostering a sense of belonging and empathy.

As you stand before Coit Tower, gazing at its exquisite form and surrounded by the panoramic beauty of San Francisco, you're reminded that every stroke of a brush and every piece of architecture can hold within it the stories, dreams, and hopes of a city and its people. Coit Tower is a tribute to the resilience of the human spirit, a symbol of the way art can shape history and inspire generations to come.

97

The Gherkin, UK

Welcome to the iconic heart of London's financial district, where the magnificent Gherkin stands as a testament to innovation and architectural brilliance. Its official name, 30 St Mary Axe, might seem formal, but its popular nickname, "The Gherkin," captures its quirky and distinctive design that has captivated both locals and visitors alike.

THE GHERKIN, UK

Completed in 2004, The Gherkin's background is rooted in a dynamic cityscape that constantly evolves. Rising 41 stories, its bold and curvaceous shape redefined London's skyline and architectural norms. Designed by the visionary architect Norman Foster, this towering marvel was crafted with sustainability in mind. Its energy-efficient glass facade maximizes natural light while minimizing heat gain, showcasing the harmony between modernity and environmental consciousness.

The Gherkin's influence is far-reaching. It's not just a building; it's a statement. Its unique design challenges the traditional notion of what a skyscraper should look like. In a city known for its historical landmarks, The Gherkin is a symbol of London's capacity to embrace the future while preserving its storied past. It's a reminder that innovation can coexist with tradition, enhancing a city's character rather than overshadowing it.

As you stand beneath The Gherkin's soaring glass curves, you're not only surrounded by its groundbreaking architecture but also by the spirit of progress and boundless human creativity. The Gherkin whispers tales of a world where imagination knows no bounds, where architects dare to dream and create structures that leave an indelible mark on both the cityscape and our collective consciousness. It serves as an inspiring beacon, inviting us all to think beyond the confines of convention and reach for the sky – quite literally.

98

The Cathedral of Brasília

THE CATHEDRAL OF BRASÍLIA

Behold the majestic Cathedral of Brasília, a true masterpiece that rises from the heart of Brazil's capital like a crystalline beacon of faith and innovation. This architectural marvel, designed by the visionary Oscar Niemeyer, stands as a testament to human creativity, blending spiritual symbolism with futuristic design.

Emerging from the imagination of Niemeyer and completed in 1970, the Cathedral of Brasília is a triumph of modernist architecture. Its ethereal form resembles a crown of thorns or hands reaching upward in prayer, inviting both believers and admirers of art to contemplate its philosophical significance. The cathedral's innovative construction defies gravity, as its 16 curved pillars create a feeling of weightlessness, inspiring visitors to transcend earthly concerns and embrace a sense of spirituality.

Niemeyer's design was a radical departure from traditional cathedrals, and its influence is profound. The Cathedral of Brasília redefines how we perceive sacred spaces, blending the sacred and the contemporary. It stands as a reminder that spirituality can find expression in daring and unexpected forms. Beyond its religious significance, the cathedral has become a cultural icon, symbolizing the aspirations of a young and vibrant nation.

As you step into the luminous interior, sunlight filtering through its breathtaking stained glass windows bathes the space in a kaleidoscope of colors. It's a sanctuary of serenity, where artistry and faith intertwine to uplift the human spirit. The Cathedral of Brasília invites us to reflect on the boundless possibilities of architecture – a language that speaks to our souls and connects us to the past, the present, and the future.

99

Shanghai World Financial Center, China

SHANGHAI WORLD FINANCIAL CENTER, CHINA

Behold the awe-inspiring Shanghai World Financial Center, a true testament to human ingenuity that pierces the sky with its distinctive and futuristic form. This iconic skyscraper, affectionately known as "The Bottle Opener" due to its unique shape, stands as a symbol of Shanghai's meteoric rise as a global financial and cultural hub.

Completed in 2008, the Shanghai World Financial Center stands as a modern marvel of architecture and engineering. Its design, reminiscent of a giant gleaming prism, exudes elegance and strength. At its heart is a circular aperture, a striking feature that gives the building its playful nickname. This design embodies a profound philosophy – it's as if the building is opening itself up to the world, inviting innovation, collaboration, and progress.

Rising to a towering height of 1,614 feet (492 meters), the Shanghai World Financial Center isn't just about impressive numbers. Its innovative design incorporates sustainable features, from energy-efficient lighting to wind-deflecting systems that ensure stability in the city's often gusty climate. The tower's influence extends beyond its physical presence – it's a representation of Shanghai's global ambitions, a hub that welcomes business, culture, and connections from all corners of the world.

As you stand before this breathtaking monument of modernity, gazing up at its shimmering façade that reflects the ever-changing cityscape, you can't help but feel a sense of wonder. The Shanghai World Financial Center isn't just a building; it's a beacon of progress, a symbol of aspiration, and a tribute to human creativity and determination. It stands as a testament to our capacity to shape the future and reach new heights – both architecturally and as a global community.

100

Fairmont Le Château Frontenac, Canada

Imagine a place where history and elegance converge in a breathtaking dance, giving birth to the magnificent Fairmont Le Château Frontenac. This iconic castle-like hotel, perched regally atop a hill in the heart of Quebec City, is not just a building – it's a living testament to time, culture, and the art of hospitality.

With a history that dates back over a century, Le Château Frontenac has witnessed the passage of time and the stories of generations. Its grandeur is rooted in its unique design, resembling a majestic medieval fortress. As you stroll through its corridors and admire its turrets and steep roofs, you're transported to a world of enchantment, where fairy tales come to life.

The innovative architecture of Le Château Frontenac was conceived by Bruce Price, an architect who sought to create a symbol of elegance that would complement the charm of Old Quebec. Today, this historic masterpiece stands as a haven for travelers seeking not just accommodation, but an experience that bridges the past with the present.

Le Château Frontenac's influence reaches beyond its walls. It's a living piece of history that has welcomed world leaders, celebrities, and adventurers from every corner of the globe. It has served as a backdrop for countless stories, celebrations, and moments that have shaped the course of time. As you stand before its magnificent façade, you can't help but feel a connection to the past – a past that is intertwined with the present, as guests from around the world continue to make memories within its storied walls.

In a world where change is constant, Le Château Frontenac stands as a reminder of the beauty of tradition, the importance of preserving our heritage, and the magic of creating timeless experiences. It's more than a building; it's a living embodiment of the human spirit's desire to create beauty, to honor the past, and to embrace the future with open arms.

Printed in Great Britain
by Amazon